UNDERSTANDING CAPITALISM

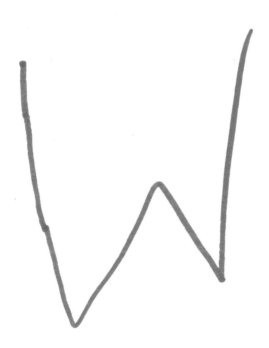

UNDERSTANDING CAPITALISM

Critical analysis from Karl Marx to Amartya Sen

Edited and introduced by

Douglas Dowd

Pluto  Press
LONDON • STERLING, VIRGINIA

First published 2002 by Pluto Press
345 Archway Road, London N6 5AA
and 22883 Quicksilver Drive, Sterling, VA 20166-2012, USA

www.plutobooks.com

British Library Cataloguing in Publication Data
A catalogue record for this book is available from the British Library

ISBN   0 7453 1783 9 hardback
ISBN   0 7453 1782 0 paperback

Library of Congress Cataloging-in-Publication Data
Understanding capitalism : critical analysis from Karl Marx to
Amartya Sen / edited and introduced by Douglas Dowd.
p. cm.
Includes bibliographical references and index.
ISBN 0–7453–1783–9 — ISBN 0–7453–1782–0 (pbk.)
1. Capitalism—History—19th century. 2. Capitalism—History—20th
century. I. Dowd, Douglas Fitzgerald, 1919–
HB501.U5643 2002
330.12′2—dc21
2001006763

10 9 8 7 6 5 4 3 2 1

Designed, typeset and produced for Pluto Press by
Chase Publishing Services, Fortescue, Sidmouth EX10 9QG
Printed and bound in the European Union by
Antony Rowe Ltd, Chippenham, England

CONTENTS

INTRODUCTION

Douglas Dowd

WHAT WE SEEK TO DO

Consider these famous observations of Karl Marx, written about 150 years ago:

> The ruling ideas of any epoch are the ideas of its ruling class; that is, the class which is the ruling *material* force of society, is at the same time its ruling *intellectual* force.
>
> It is not the consciousness of men that determines their being, but, on the contrary, their social being that determines their consciousness.[1]

It is extraordinary that these epigrams have retained their applicability up to our time, given the subsequent emergence and contemporary prevalence of political democracy; that in fact they now have considerably more force than when first uttered is due not only to Marx's acuity but to the manner in which the seemingly unlimited powers of contemporary capitalism have managed to exploit not just workers and nature, but, as well, the inherent limits of (to adapt a phrase) "currently existing democracy."

Capital's powers, that is, are considerably greater than in the nineteenth century; so much so, indeed, that in the U.S., the most capitalist and the most powerful ever of any society, the very term "class" has lost its earlier invidious and combative connotations: factory workers, miners, farmers, entrepreneurs – "the butchers, the bakers, the candlestick makers" – all but the very rich and the very poor – have learned to see themselves as they have come to be described, as members of the "middle class." As in so many other important socioeconomic matters, other capitalist nations, although lagging, trod along the same path.

At least as striking is that in the many decades after Marx wrote, and ending (if only for a while) in 1945, the social process was like a raging river, with the entire world intermittently in turmoil – mainly consequent upon capitalism's deepening and spread, and the opposition to it. The vast human, economic and social devastation from the two global wars marking that process also yielded ubiquitous social exhaustion – except for the United States; but all that also produced a set of opportunities to start afresh. Some of those opportunities were at least partially realized in the two decades or so after the war; since the 1970s, they have gone into reverse.

Their realization required and allowed that the practice of political democracy would go beyond voting Tweedledee or Tweedledum to include movement toward economic and social democracy – as with workers' ability to gain strong economically and politically influential unions to improve their wages and working conditions and gain a "social wage," the lessening of racial and gender discrimination and, *inter alia*, improved security and comfort for the old and disabled.

However, with the onset of pervasive socioeconomic crises in the 1970s – economically marked by a decade-long persistence of combined rising unemployment *and* severe inflation – capital was able to achieve a dramatic reversal of that progress. They did so in a set of processes aptly dubbed the "corporate counterattack."[2] In consequence, capital's power today is less challenged than in the nineteenth century. That power holds sway in different forms now than earlier, as will soon be noted; but, both earlier and now, economics has rationalized both the means and ends of capital – and, in doing so, has lent dignity and reason to what otherwise would have to be seen as one combination of another of the "seven deadly sins."[3]

The "different forms" are many; most vital are those having to do with the sheer size of today's monstrous transnational companies: in 2000, the 500 largest global corporations had combined revenues over $14 trillion; the largest 10 among them had revenues exceeding $1.6 trillion (with profits of $84 billion).[4]

The powers of such companies go beyond production and trade into every crevice of social existence: into the politics, the culture, into every thought and feeling in all social spheres; as they must, if their "ideas" are to preside over our lives – as indeed they do, as never before. How so?

It is common and reasonable enough to point to the interacting role of the media and of consumerism in that evolution, and all the more so as we approach the present. But the media – whether the reference is to print, radio, TV, to "news" or to entertainment – are the *transmitter* not the *originator* of those "ruling ideas."

The ensuing essays serve as critiques of one vital set of *originators*, that is, with ideas developed predominantly by economists in universities. There, in both past and present, usually unconsciously, "the ideas of the ruling class" have been absorbed and transformed. They take the form of "economic theory," which in turn is translated into economic policy prescriptions accepted, adapted, and utilized by those in the realms of business, government, journalism and the reading public. There has always been dissent, of course; it has rarely been effective for any but short periods, here and there. Thus, it is very difficult for members of the concerned public or even for students of economics to find reasoned alternatives to the *status quo*.

That is so today, even as political dissent rises, most especially as concerns "globalization." Irrespective of the broad-based nature of the participants in that dissent – whether as expressed in Seattle, or Gothenburg, or Genoa, in left of center periodicals or the occasional book – all reasoning against today's euphemism for capitalism, "the free market," is quickly and loudly dismissed as one form or another of juvenile or hysterical or misguided well-intentioned ideas. Or something.

The aim of this book is to show, instead, how misguided and not only useless but downright harmful mainstream economics has been, is, and always more becomes. Just how systematic this domination is seen when it is noted that when – as happened with Keynes, for example – once a *leader* of that economics provides an alternative view in time of severe crisis (the 1930s depression in his case), the contribution faces strong opposition from the beginning, and, if and when it manages to take hold, is relegated to the garbage dump at the very first opportunity.[5]

Our book was written for those who, puzzled or upset by the functioning of the socioeconomy, need and want to have a surer grasp of capitalism's realities. It is entirely justifiable to expect that economists would answer at least these questions: (1) what do we need to know about the economy? (2) What must be done in order that the economy better serve human, social, and environmental needs?

However, far from answering such questions, mainstream economists in practice prevent them from being asked. One can gain a PhD in Economics in the United States and, while learning a great deal of economic *theory*, never learn *any*thing about the economy. Worse, governmental economic policies all too often use that same economic theory as their rationale for harmful socioeconomic policies; and, increasingly, both such economics and policies are taking place elsewhere.

If economics provided what is expected of it, a book such as this would be unnecessary; lamentably, the intricate webs of economists' abstractions give us something very much like the opposite. Our essays seek to counteract those contrived and harmful misunderstandings: (a) by bringing back to life and "updating" important contributions from the relatively distant past (on Marx, Veblen, and Gramsci) and (b) by pulling back from the shadows the valuable contributions of more recent and of contemporary "heterodox" or radical economists that have been ignored, neglected, distorted, or forgotten.

Brought to bear on today's political economy, all these can nourish understanding – as could (and have) other essays on those same thinkers, and on others from the past and present.[6]

Suffice it to say in this brief introduction that whatever other value this book may have, it will show that mainstream economics, far from being the "science" it claims to be, serves instead as capitalism's ideology. In our day, in addition to the other sources of power possessed by those who rule, that of today's mammoth corporations is inordinately strengthened by its ability to have its ideology become an integral part of our socialization processes, polluting economics as much as the air we breathe.

Irrespective of which thinkers are discussed in the essays, the emphasis will be on the contemporary economy. As will be briefly noted here (and elaborated upon later), the functioning of that economy consists of and depends upon much of what mainstream economic theory considers to be "non-economic" – so irrelevant in fact that to be ignorant of it is "no problem." This stance is not a consequence of sheer stupidity; it is, rather, the predictable outcome of the aims and means, the whys and wherefores of mainstream economic theory. Sustained attention will be given to those matters of "methodology" in the essays; here we remark only that to *become* a "mainstream economist" entails a rigorous training that *systematically* excludes from focus virtually all of what needs to be examined; or, as Veblen put it more than a century ago, "to be an economist is to have developed a trained *in*capacity" to comprehend the vital elements of the socioeconomic process. And today's economic theorists are even more ignorant than in his time. Now a short comment on the foregoing generalizations.

THE DERELICTIONS OF ECONOMICS

What then do mainstream economists do? First and foremost (and, increasingly, only) they learn economic theory, the seat of the analytical "brains trust" of economics. That theory studies, or, more accurately, abstractly posits the characteristics of, certain segments of the economic process: (a) commodity markets ("microeconomics"), (b) the expansion/contraction of the economy as a whole ("macroeconomics"), (c) the economic relationships between nations ("trade theory"), and (d) the determinants of wages, interest, profits, and rent ("distribution theory"). At what is seen as their highest level, these theories are integrated as the theory of general equilibrium – ignoring the clear and important truth that economic life takes place over historical/irreversible time, not in Newtonian space.

To repeat: what is "studied" in all these respects are not the relevant areas of reality, but the posited/imagined relationships between abstract symbols purporting to represent relationships within and between (for example) demand and supply (in one variation or another). Whether the equational manipulations involved are on a low or a high level, in all cases they begin and end with the "examination" of unreal relationships enclosed in always tinier cubicles – like prisoners; and, like prisoners, those in a given "cubicle" cannot, in principle, communicate with those in the others.

Let us be clear: the problem is not with either abstraction or specialization as such; both are essential for understanding (physical and social) reality: "If appearance and reality were identical, there would be no need for theory," as Marx pointed out. (The sun appears to revolve around the earth; to know that it does not, Copernicus showed, requires more than observation.)

Rather, the problem with economics arises from its principles of selection, which questions it asks and – at least as important – does *not* ask, what is abstracted from and what is and is *not* focused upon, and *why* – or, ultimately, saying something like the same thing, who gains and who loses from the policies flowing from the theory.

Economic theory in principle abstracts from reality not only in some, but in *all* vital respects – from history, social institutions (not least in importance, the structures, sources and uses of power), from technology, and (among other matters) from the "surrounding" natural environment.

It dignifies this charade by a linguistic curtsey, *ceteris paribus* – meaning "other things being equal" – those "other things" presumably to be brought back into the analysis when necessary: but that time quite simply *never* comes (and were it, most economists would not know, or would have forgotten, what the "other things" ever were). Having blithely brushed all of complicating reality under the rug, economics then proceeds to provide the theoretical bases for idealized "free markets."

Early in the past century, the eminent mainstream "methodologist," Sir Lionel Robbins, put forth the definition of economics that persists to this day: "Economics is the science of allocating scarce means to unlimited wants," agreeing, if not in these words, that "free markets" ensure the best possible allocation, for the good of all. In the long run.

As will be seen at some length in our essays, "means" (human and other natural resources) are *not* scarce, and "wants" are *not* unlimited. In reality, human resources are wantonly *under*used or despoiled, and other natural resources (most flagrantly, petroleum) are dangerously and recklessly *over*used; and as for "wants," rather than being unlimited, business long ago discovered both the necessity and the means for "creating" wants, now a major industry.

Some of this will be shown in the chapters to follow, where it will be seen that "wants" are not the same thing as "needs" – human, social, or environmental – and that the very word "need" quite simply does not occur in economic theory.

As to the freedom of markets, it defies reason in this world of supercorporations to see markets as "free" – when, for example, in the U.S. the 500 largest industrial companies (out of millions) normally do about 80 per cent of all sales, with the *ten* largest alone taking 30 per cent. The "freedom" so much touted is Orwellian, where "free" refers to the freedom of giant companies to do as they please. Not quite what Adam Smith had in mind.

You don't have to be an economist – indeed it's better not to be one – to know that what we call "economic" activities take place *over time* in a complex set of relationships both within and between societies – an interacting mix of economic, political, sociocultural, technological, psychological and (among others) military processes and relationships. To abstract from (that is, pay no attention to) such a set of complexities is to place the possibilities of understanding permanently beyond reach – and, at the same time, to put in place misinformation and systematic confusions which, while and because they obfuscate reality, facilitate the easy maintenance of a social system that distorts and crushes human possibilities and destroys its natural base.

It is worth noting that when economics began, whatever was wrong with it, it was not nearly as shameless in its procedures as now. It was born as a discipline just as (and because) capitalism and the possibilities of modern industry were taking their first secure hold. That was in Britain in the late eighteenth century, with Adam Smith (1723–1790) and his *Wealth of Nations* (1776). Emerging at the same time was the socioeconomic philosophy of Jeremy Bentham (1748–1832), in his *Introduction to the Principles of Morals and Legislation* (1780), and its "utilitarianism." The most important subsequent work was that of David Ricardo (1772–1823), with his *Principles of Political Economy and Taxation* (1815).

Taken together those works constituted the foundations of "classical political economy." That began to be replaced in the 1860s by "neoclassical economics," the continuing theoretical framework of today's "economics." Standing on those foundations are today's doctrines hailing the virtues of the "free market" within and between nations and the presumed "rationality" that guides the behavior of consumers, businesses, and workers.

Classical political economy (as developed by those just noted, and subsequently) deserved and received criticism as industrial capitalism proceeded – from "outside," as with Marx, and from "inside," as with John Stuart Mill (1806–1873); and both sets of critiques may be seen as just.

Smith and his successors however were writing in the very youth of industrial capitalism; and even though Smith, Bentham, and Ricardo were explictly aware of – and accepted – the exploitation and disruptions of industrial capitalism, they could not see what its "healthy" functioning would entail by the late nineteenth century (let alone by our own time). Such as? The short-list includes the direct and "collateral damages" of the socioeconomic disruptions repeating and going well beyond those of Britain's industrial revolution – whether on the Continent or in the United States or Japan, to say nothing of what was also entailed by the transformation of colonialism (and its massive horrors) to the considerably deeper penetrations and socio/cultural/political/economic devastation wrought by its successor, imperialism. And, today, globalization.

Nor did Smith et al. foresee the giant corporations extant by 1900, let alone the megagiants of our own time. As for Bentham and his "psychological hedonism" and its rationalities, it is not necessary to glorify the "science of psychology" today to accept that in his day, there was nothing but inspired guesses.

Nonetheless, as will be noted in later pages, already by the end of the nineteenth century there was a well-developed and rapidly developing literature of criticism and awareness, whether as regards the plight of workers, the rise of big business and imperialism, or psychology (among other matters). As will be seen in Chapter 2, Thorstein Veblen exemplified that set of possibilities in his own substantial writings, regarding, most relevantly for present purposes, the major tendencies of the late nineteenth century (along with great prescience for our time) and the deep shortcomings of economics.

In 1909 Veblen published an essay taunting the central theoretical device of the then (and still) ruling and devising "neoclassical economics," a scathing critique of utility theory and its Benthamite psychological underpinnings. An excerpt seems a fitting way to close this discussion. As you read along, note that all relationships are spatial and that time plays no role – very much the opposite of economic reality – and remember that, despite all, what Veblen satirized then beats still as the heart of "demand and supply" economics:

> The hedonistic conception of man is that of a lightning calculator of pleasures and pains, who oscillates like a homogeneous globule of desire of happiness under the impulse of stimuli that shift him about the area, but leave him intact. He has neither antecedent nor consequent. He is an isolated, definitive human datum, in stable equilibrium except for the buffets of the impinging forces that displace him in one direction or another. Self-imposed in elemental space, he spins symmetrically about his own spiritual axis until the parallelogram of forces bears down upon him, whereupon he follows the line of the resultant. When the force of the impact is spent, he comes to rest, a self-contained globule of desire as before.[7]

To sum up, what is wrong in mainstream economics is not that it theorizes, but the Alice in Wonderland view of an economy that it posits: an economy floating pleasantly through space, unconnected to its – or any – universe, producing the best of all possible worlds for all, somehow, somewhere, some time: a cheerleader's view of social reality.

As such, economics performs as ideology. Whether its purveyors know what they're doing or not, is not important: what they do is harmful, what they do not do but that others have done and do, badly needs recognition and study. This book seeks to assist in that process.

Here now is a short synopsis of the essays, in the order in which they appear. At the end of the book there is a brief note concerning each of the authors.

THE ESSAYS

The works on which these essays are based go back to the mid-nineteenth century and up to the present. The contributors are mostly economists (Hahnel, Keaney, Lebowitz, Lee and myself), but one is a sociologist (Foster) and another is a political scientist (Boggs), a mix befitting a book that seeks to add to the understanding of capitalism – which is, after all, not just an economic but a social system. Indeed, as will be seen in what follows, capitalism could not have come into existence, let alone have endured, unless its reach extended well beyond those two abstractions: the "economy" and "markets."

Chapter 1 Karl Marx (1818–1883)
The depth and breadth of Marx's writings cannot of course be represented in an essay (or in several books). Michael Lebowitz has chosen to take as his starting-point Marx's truly soaring conception of human potentialities. From there, he explores Marx's analysis of the structure and dynamics of capitalism, noting both the endless and heedless drive of capital which, by its very nature, inexorably stunts human development; and he compares those realities with the drives and the needs of human beings for their own development.

In pursuing those analyses, Lebowitz also underscores the sharp contrast between the historical and holistic framework within which Marx worked and the "atomistic," ahistorical and asocial procedures of neoclassical economics.

Chapter 2 Thorstein Veblen (1857–1929)
An old joke concerning a certain writer put it that "he's been writing prose without knowing it." That is also true as regards Marx and Veblen: much of what many serious social analysts take for granted derives, whether they know it or not, from Marx and/or Veblen. Most of what Veblen wrote was truly

original, but it may be doubted that he would have looked at, or seen, much of what he did had he not been a very serious reader of the Marxian corpus.

Although Veblen acknowledged Marx as the very most useful of the political economists, he was also Marx's strong – if friendly – critic; as will also be seen, Veblen regularly sought to camouflage what many have nonetheless seen as his radicalism.

Veblen came to maturity half a century after Marx, and in the U.S., as will be emphasized in the chapter. In that half-century, early industrialism had become full industrialism, with a substantially more advanced technology; and it had become "full" not in relatively tiny England (the sole industrial power, then) but in the enormous United States, and in another and extraordinarily different world: several industrial societies (the U.S., Germany, Japan), soon, if not already, to be leaving Britain behind.

Those differences were among others decisive in shaping Veblen's analyses: (1) his methodological critiques were aimed at neoclassical economics, not, as with Marx, at classical political economy; (2) he took for granted the "technology of physics and chemistry" and socioeconomic domination by big business and monopoly, rather than, as with Marx, assuming competitive structures (prescient though he was about the future of both technology and big business); and, among other matters, (3) Veblen understood already in 1904 (in his *Theory of Business Enterprise*) that the conflict between capital and labor would favor capital through its ability to exploit the irrationalities in us (as regards nationalism, racism, and greed), having, as they did already in Veblen's time, controlled access to what would become the modern media.

Chapter 3 **What Gramsci Means Today**
Gramsci has long been a "household name" in Italy, and very well-known in most of Europe; in the United States he was virtually unknown until well after World War II. The work of Carl Boggs was vital in introducing English-speaking readers to this seminal thinker, beginning with his *Gramsci's Marxism* (1976).

As World War I ended, Gramsci was becoming the leading Marxist–Leninist thinker in Italy; by 1924 he had become the most effective *critic* of the Leninist politics, while remaining a Marxist in his political economy. In his chapter, Boggs takes several of Gramsci's main concepts as they relate to contemporary capitalism and the contemporary left. Among the Gramscian concepts to be pursued and evaluated (and which must await definition until the essay) are "ideological hegemony," "social bloc," "war of position," "modern prince," "prefigurative struggles," and "the organic intellectual." To the degree that his essay succeeds in its aims, Boggs will help to establish "a kind of dialectic" between what Gramsci was writing about (while in a fascist prison), the Italy of his time, and the historical situation in which we find ourselves today.

Chapter 4 **Critical Institutionalism: from American exceptionalism to international relevance**
"Institutionalist" is a term whose origin goes back to Veblen (although he did not classify himself as such), because he made so much of the importance of "institutions" in shaping socioeconomic processes. Simply put, the term refers to the ways in which we organize our lives (or have them organized for us), and our linked habits of thought and feeling. Thus marriage is an institution, as is banking, as is driving on one side of the road rather than the other, as is private property, as is the death penalty (or its absence).

Institutionalists emphasize the evolutionary nature of economy and society and therefore stress the importance of historical relevance. The U.S. Institutionalist tradition of thought comprises an eclectic group of dissenters whose dissatisfaction with conventional economics has inspired both important critique and policy alternatives – although its members are not found on any one part of the political spectrum.

In his chapter, Michael Keaney describes the antecedents of Institutionalism, and goes on to examine the contributions of key contributors such as J.R. Commons, C.E. Ayres, Robert A. Brady, John Kenneth Galbraith and Marc Tool. It will be seen that there are certain commonalities between U.S. Institutionalism and, say, the Historical school of Europe.

Chapter 5 *Post Keynesian Economics (1930–2000): an emerging heterodox theory of capitalism*

This school of economic thought has been emerging with ever-increasing strength for the past few decades. Its "name" can be misleading, for Keynes himself, in his *General Theory of Employment, Interest and Money* was concerned entirely with "macroeconomic" analysis. Much of an advance over mainstream economics though that was, however, it was limited by two major problems: (1) its theoretical framework employed the same set of abstractions as neoclassical economics as regards both macro and micro matters, with Keynes altering only one assumption (that having to do with savings); (2) it did not do what the Post Keynesians (hereafter: PKs) seek to do; namely, to develop an analysis integrating macro, micro, trade and distribution theory. Among the many positive differences thus achieved, not least in importance is that the PKs are able to include in their analyses questions of socioeconomic power, the omission of which from *The General Theory* has been most damaging.

Frederic Lee begins his essay on those origins, and a brief history of the always changing group's history in the U.K. and the U.S. He goes on to show how the content of PK economics has changed over its development, by incorporating material from institutional, social and radical economics.

Turning to the present Lee outlines current PK micro and macro theory; he concludes with a discussion of how PK analysis facilitates our understanding of capitalism, its social democratic policy proposals, and its approach to issues of antitrust. His final section argues that PK theory can be distinctly radical, and that its analyses may be interpreted to conclude that capitalism cannot be made more acceptable, but must be replaced.

Chapter 6 *Paul Sweezy and Monopoly Capital*

In 1949, Paul Sweezy and Leo Huberman began the publication of their "independent socialist magazine" *The Monthly Review*.

In 1953 (in order to publish I.F. Stone's *Hidden History of the Korean War*, which no U.S. publisher would accept) they established the Monthly Review Press; in 1966 the press published *Monopoly Capital: An Essay on the American Economic and Social Order*, by Paul Baran (who died before its publication) and Paul Sweezy.

At that time Baran and Sweezy were the two most prominent Marxists in the United States, perhaps in the English-speaking world. The modifications they sought to make in Marxian analysis were well-suggested by the book's title: "Monopoly Capital," "American," and "Economic *and* Social Order" – as distinct from Marx's "Capital" (and its assumptions of a competitive economy), his focus on (a) Britain, and (b) production.

John Bellamy Foster begins his essay by paying attention to the tidal waves of megamergers accompanying globalization, and their sharp contrast with contemporary neoliberal perspectives on the economy; he then refers back to the rise of big business ("monopoly capital") a century ago. This takes him to Marx's views on the concentration and centralization of capital, and thus to Baran and Sweezy's *Monopoly Capital*, the main focus of the essay. As relevant, he notes earlier contributions in this area made by thinkers such as Lenin, Kalecki, Steindl, Kolko, and others.

Chapter 7 **Amartya Sen (1933–)**
Amartya Sen stands in contrast with all the others considered in our book: he does not yet stand for a "school," is as much a professional philosopher as a professional economist (having held chairs for both disciplines at both Harvard and Oxford), and is an Asian; and, most relevantly for our purposes, Sen, although a "welfare economics theorist," has spent his long professional career focusing on what in this world should, but rarely if ever does, command the attention of his fellow welfare economists: poverty, famine and hunger, and the roots of unwanted population growth resulting from the combination of poverty and the oppression of women over much of the world: in sum, his work has homed in on the relationships between global inequalities and the denial of human needs.

Robin Hahnel's chapter details Sen's contribution to our understanding of these vital matters – an understanding inseparable from an understanding of capitalism.

NOTES

1. The first was written (with Engels) in 1844, in *The German Ideology*, the second in 1859, in the Preface to *A Contribution to the Critique of Political Economy*. Both may be found in *Selected Works of Marx and Engels* (International Publishers, 1967).

2. The term is that of Richard B. Du Boff, found in his excellent *Accumulation and Power: An Economic History of the United States* (New York: M.E. Sharpe, Inc., 1989). What was underway in the U.S. was also taking hold elsewhere; indeed, its most prominent early successes were in Great Britain, with the triumphant upsurge of Conservatism, led by Margaret Thatcher.

3. Which are, in case you have forgotten, anger, envy, gluttony, avarice, lust, pride, and sloth. Traces of all these are doubtless found in all of us: it is contemporary capitalism's victory to have utilized advertising to tease them out of us, and lead us to ape our rulers in their practice, in one combination or another. As will be seen in Chapter 2, over a century ago Thorstein Veblen saw this as capitalism's trump card – trumping, that is, workers' inclination to organize for their common interests with what Veblen called "emulation," seeking to be like rather than to overthrow their rulers.

4. *Fortune Magazine*, July 23, 2001. *Fortune* annually provides this information for the largest global companies, the largest U.S. companies, and other such measures, showing revenues, profits, assets, and numbers of employees, along with other useful information, in diverse issues coming out in the spring and early summer. Worth noting is that of the Top Ten, five were auto companies and three were oil companies (the other two were General Electric and Wal-Mart – the latter now the second (to Exxon Mobil) largest company in the world, with (except for two Chinese companies) the most employees: 1.2 million).

5. In the case of Keynes, and his *General Theory of Employment, Interest and Money* (1936) it was only adopted seriously in one country before World War II, and that was in Nazi Germany, where it came into being as what is called and is practiced as "military Keynesianism" in the United States. Many of Keynes's most beneficially useful ideas, those which he saw as central, were adopted wholeheartedly in Western Europe after the war, and less so in the U.S.: they are now termed "left-wing Keynesianism."

6. Putting together a collection such as this understandably suffers from such problems of choice. But at least recommendations can be made concerning others whose ideas not only would fit with the intent of this book, but which have inspired others, including many of the recent economists discussed here. Here we may note four such economists and provide references to some excellent works concerning them: Joan Robinson, Michael Kalecki, Maurice Dobb and Piero Sraffa, all of whom (although Kalecki was born in Poland and Sraffa in Italy) spent all or most of their lives working in Britain.

Rima, Ingrid H. (1991) *The Joan Robinson Legacy* (Armonk, NY: M.E. Sharpe).

Feiwel, George R. (1975) *The Intellectual Capital of Michael Kalecki: A Study in Economic Theory and Policy* (Knoxville, TE: University of Tennessee Press).

Feinstein, C.H. (1967) *Socialism, Capitalism and Economic Growth: Essays Presented to Maurice Dobb* (Cambridge: Cambridge University Press).

Potier, Jean-Pierre (1991) *Piero Sraffa: Unorthodox Economist* (London: Routledge).

It may also be added that Robinson and Kalecki both helped Keynes with his *General Theory*, and that their works were integral to what became Post Keynesianism; and that Amartya Sen, one of those considered in this book, studied with both Dobb and Sraffa.

7. The article was "The Limitations of Marginal Utility," and it is found in a collection of Veblen's essays entitled *The Place of Science in Modern Civilization* (New York: B.W. Huebsch, 1919).

1 KARL MARX:
The Needs of Capital vs.
The Needs of Human Beings [1]

Michael A. Lebowitz

Like other early nineteenth-century socialists, Karl Marx's vision of the good society was one that would unleash the full development of all human potential. "What is the aim of the Communists?" asked Marx's comrade Friedrich Engels in his early draft of the *Communist Manifesto*. "To organise society in such a way that every member of it can develop and use all his capabilities and powers in complete freedom and without thereby infringing the basic conditions of this society." In Marx's final version of the *Manifesto*, that new society appears as an "association, in which the free development of each is the condition for the free development of all."[2]

This idea of the development of human potential runs throughout Marx's work – the possibility of rich human beings with rich human needs, the potential for producing human beings as rich as possible in needs and capabilities. What, indeed, is wealth, he asked, "other than the universality of individual needs, capacities, pleasures, productive forces...?" Think about the "development of the rich individuality which is as all-sided in its production as in its consumption"; think about "the absolute working-out of his creative potentialities." The real goal is the "development of all human powers as such the end in itself."

Realization of this potential, however, cannot drop from the sky. It requires the development of a society in which people do not look upon each other as separate, one where we consciously recognize our interdependence and freely cooperate upon the basis of that recognition. When we relate to each other as human beings, Marx proposed, we produce for each other simply because we understand that others need the results of our activity, and we get pleasure and satisfaction from the knowledge that we are accomplishing something worthwhile. Your need would be sufficient to ensure my activity, and, in responding, I would be "confirmed both in your thought and your love." What Marx was describing, of course, is the concept of a human family.

Marx's vision of a society of freely associated producers, a profoundly moral and ethical one, led him quite early in his life to pose certain analytical questions. What is it about this society in which we now live that, if you were to tell me you had a need for something I was capable of satisfying, it would be considered as a plea, a humiliation, "and consequently uttered with a feeling of shame, of degradation?" Why is it, he asked, that rather than affirming that I am capable of activity that helps another human being, your needs are instead a source of power for me? "Far from being the *means* which would give you *power* over my production, they [your needs] are instead the *means* for giving me power over you."

As long as we relate to one another not as members of a human community but as self-seeking owners, Marx concluded, this perverted separation of people is constantly reproduced. So, Marx was led to explore the nature of the social relations that exist between people, the character of the relations in which they engage in producing – producing themselves as well as producing for each other. It was how he proceeded to analyze capitalism.

CAPITALIST RELATIONS OF PRODUCTION

The story told by economists who celebrate capitalism is that competition and markets ensure that capitalists will satisfy the needs of people – not because of their humanity and benevolence but (as Adam Smith put it) "from a regard to their own interest." Competing on the market with other capitalists, they are driven (as if whipped by an invisible hand) to serve the people. For Marx, though, this focus upon competition and markets obscures exactly what distinguishes capitalism from other market economies – its specific relations of production. There are two central aspects of capitalist relations of production – the side of capitalists and the side of workers. On the one hand, there are capitalists – the owners of wealth, the owners of the physical and material means of production. Their orientation is toward the growth of their wealth. Beginning with capital of a certain value in the form of money, capitalists purchase commodities with the goal of gaining *more* money, additional value, surplus value: and that's the point, profits. As capitalists, all that matters for them is the growth of their capital.

On the other hand, we have workers – people who have neither material goods they can sell nor the material means of producing the things they need for themselves. Without those means of production, they cannot produce commodities to sell in the market to exchange. So, how do they get the things they need? By selling the only thing they do have to sell, their ability to work. They can sell it to whomever they choose, but they cannot choose *whether or not* to sell their power to perform labor … if they are to survive.

Before we can talk about capitalism, in short, certain conditions must already be present. Not only must there be a commodity–money economy in which some people are the owners of means of production but also there must be a special commodity available on the market – the capacity to perform labor. For that to happen, Marx proposed, workers first must be free in a double sense. They must be free to sell their labor-power (i.e., have property rights in their capacity to perform labor – something the slave, for example, lacks) and they must be "free" of means of production (i.e., the means of production must have been separated from producers). In other words, one aspect unique to capitalist relations of production is that it is characterized by the existence of people who, lacking the means of production, are able and compelled to sell a property right, the right of disposition over their ability to work. They are compelled to sell their power to produce in order to get money to buy the things they need.

Nevertheless, it is important to understand that, while the separation of the means of production from producers is a necessary condition for capitalist relations of production, it is not a sufficient condition. If workers are separated from the means of production, there remain two possibilities: (1) workers sell their labor-power to the owners of means of production or (2) workers rent means of production from their owners. There is a long tradition in mainstream economics which proposes that it does not matter whether capital hires labor or labor hires capital because the results will be the same in both cases. For Marx, we will see, there was a profound difference: only the first case, where the sale of labor-power occurs, is capitalism; only there do we see the unique characteristics of capitalism.

However, it is not simply wage-labor that is critical. Capitalism requires both the existence of labor-power as a commodity and its combination with *capital*. Who buys that particular property right in the market and why? The capitalist buys the right to dispose of the worker's capacity to perform labor precisely because it is a means to achieve *his* goal, profits. Because that and only that, the growth of his capital, is what interests him as a capitalist.

Well, we now have the basis for an exchange between two parties in the market, the owner of money and the owner of labor-power. Each of them wants what the other has; each gets something out of that exchange. It looks like a free transaction. This is the point at which most non-Marxist economics stops. It looks at the transactions that take place in the market, and it declares, "we see freedom." This is what Marx described as "the realm of Freedom, Equality, Property, and Bentham." In fact, since the "free-trader *vulgaris*" sees *only* the transactions in the marketplace, he sees only freedom.

But this is not *every* market economy we are describing here. Not every market economy is characterized by the sale of labor-power to a capitalist. A defense of a market economy as such is not a defense of capitalism, any more than a defense of the market is a defense of slavery (which of course involved the buying and selling of slaves). This distinction between capitalism and markets, is not one, however, the defenders of capitalism tend to make – their ideology, Marx proposed, leads them to confuse on principle the characteristics of pre-capitalist market economies with capitalism.

Why? Think about what is unique about this market

economy in which labor-power has been sold to the capitalist. Now that the market transaction is over, Marx commented, we see that something has happened to each of the two parties. "He who was previously the money-owner now strides out in front as a capitalist; the possessor of labor-power follows as his worker." And where are they going? They are entering the place of work; they are entering the place where the capitalist now has the opportunity to *use* that property right which he has purchased.

THE SPHERE OF CAPITALIST PRODUCTION

Two central characteristics exist in the process of production that takes place under capitalist relations. First, the worker works under the direction, supervision, and control of the capitalist. The goals of the capitalist determine the nature and purpose of production. Directions and orders in the production process come to workers from above. There is no horizontal relationship between capitalist and worker as buyer and seller in the marketplace here; there is no market here. Rather, there is a vertical relation between the one who has power and the one who does not. It is a command system, what Marx described as the despotism of the capitalist workplace. So much for the realm of freedom and equality.

Why does the capitalist have this power over workers here? Because he purchased the right to dispose of their ability to perform labor. That was the property right he purchased. It was the property right that the worker sold and *had* to sell because it was the only option available if they were to survive.

The second characteristic of capitalist production is that workers have no property rights in the product that results from their activity. They have no claim. They have sold to the capitalist the only thing that might have given them a claim, the capacity to perform labor. In contrast to producers in a cooperative who benefit from their own efforts because they have property rights in the products they produce, when workers work harder or more productively in the capitalist firm, they increase the value of the *capitalist's* property. Unlike a cooperative (which is not characterized by capitalist relations of production), in the capitalist firm all the fruits of the worker's productive activity belong to the capitalist, the residual claimant. This is why the sale of labor-power is so critical as a distinguishing characteristic of capitalism.

What happens, then, in the sphere of capitalist production? It all follows logically from the nature of capitalist relations of production. Insofar as the capitalist's goal is surplus value, he only purchases labor-power to the extent that it will generate that surplus value. For Marx, the necessary condition for generation of surplus value was the performance of surplus labor – the performance of labor over and above the labor contained in what the capitalist pays as wages. The capitalist, through the combination of his control of production and ownership of the product of labor, will act to ensure that workers add more value in production than the capitalist has paid them.

How does this occur? At any given point, we can calculate the hours of daily labor that are necessary to maintain workers at their existing standard of living. Those hours of "necessary labor," Marx proposed, are determined by the relationship between the existing standard of necessity (the real wage) and the general level of productivity. If productivity rises, then fewer hours of labor would be necessary for workers to reproduce themselves. Simple. Of course, the capitalist has no interest in a situation in which workers work only long enough to maintain themselves. What the capitalist wants is that workers perform *surplus* labor – that is, that the labor performed by workers (the capitalist work-day) *exceeds* the level of necessary labor. The ratio between surplus labor and necessary labor is what Marx defined as the rate of exploitation (or, in its monetary form, the rate of surplus value).

We now have in place the elements that can illustrate what Marx referred to as the "law of motion," i.e., the dynamic properties which flow from these particular capitalist relations of production. Remember that the whole purpose of the process from the point of view of the capitalist is profit. The worker is only a means to this end – the growth of capital. Let us begin with an extreme assumption – that the work-day is equal to the level of necessary labor (i.e., there is no surplus labor). If this assumption were to remain true, there would be no capitalist production. So, what can the capitalist do in order to achieve his goal?

One option for the capitalist is to use his control over production to increase the work that the laborer performs. Extend the work-day, make the work-day as long as possible. A 10-hour work-day? Fine. A 12-hour work-day? Even better. The worker will perform more work for the capitalist over and above the wage, and capital will grow. Another way is by intensifying the work-day. Speed it up. Make workers work harder and faster in a given time period. Make sure there is no wasted motion, no slack time. Every moment workers rest is time they are not working for capital.

Another option for the capitalist is to reduce what he pays. Drive down the real wage. Bring in people who will work for less. Encourage people to compete with each other to see who will work for the least. Bring in immigrants, impoverished people from the countryside. Relocate to where you can get cheap labor.

That is the inherent logic of capital. The inherent tendency of capital is to increase the exploitation of workers. In the one case, the work-day is increasing; in the other, the real wage is falling. In both cases, the rate of exploitation is driven upward. Marx commented that "the capitalist [is] constantly tending to reduce wages to their physical minimum and extend the working day to its physical maximum." He *continued*, however, by saying "while the working man constantly presses in the opposite direction."

In other words, within the framework of capitalist relations, while capital pushes to increase the work-day both in length and intensity and to drive down wages, workers struggle to reduce the work-day and to increase wages. They form trade unions for this purpose. Just as there is struggle from the side of capital, so also is there class struggle from the side of the worker. Why? Take the struggle over the work-day, for example. Why do the workers want more time for themselves? Marx refers to "time for education, for intellectual development, for the fulfillment of social functions, for social intercourse, for the free play of the vital forces of his body and his mind." Time, Marx noted, is "the room of human development. A man who has no free time to dispose of, whose whole lifetime, apart from the mere physical interruptions by sleep, meals, and so forth, is absorbed by his labor for the capitalist, is less than a beast of burden."

What about the struggle for higher wages? Of course, there are the physical requirements to survive that must be obtained. But Marx understood that workers need much more than this. The worker's social needs include "the worker's participation in the higher, even cultural satisfactions, the agitation for his own interests, newspaper subscriptions, attending lectures, educating his children, developing his taste, etc." In short, workers have their own goals. As they are beings within society, their needs are necessarily socially determined. Their needs as human beings within society stand opposite capital's own inherent tendencies in production. When we look at the side of the worker, we recognize, as Marx did, "the worker's own need for development."

From the perspective of capital, though, workers and, indeed, all human beings, are only means to an end. They are not an end in themselves. If satisfying the goals of capital requires employing racism, dividing workers, using the state to outlaw or crush unions, destroying people's lives and futures by shutting down operations and moving to parts of the world in which the people are poor and unions banned, so be it. Capitalism has never been a system whose priority is human beings and their needs.

True, wages have increased and the work-day has been reduced since Marx wrote, but that still doesn't invalidate Marx's description of capitalism – every gain occurs in the face of opposition from capitalists (as it did in Marx's time). Writing about the Ten-Hours Bill, the law that reduced the length of the work-day in England to ten hours, Marx described it as a great victory, a victory over "the blind rule of the supply and demand laws" which form the political economy of the capitalist class; it was the first time, he noted, that "in broad daylight the political economy of the [capitalist] class succumbed to the political economy of the working class."

In other words, the gains workers make are the result of their struggles. They press in the opposite direction to capital; they struggle to reduce the rate of exploitation. Implicit in that political economy of workers and in the struggles of working people is the overcoming of divisions among them (whatever their source). None of this is new. Marx described the hostility at the time between English and Irish workers as the source of their weakness: "It is the secret by which the capitalist class maintains its power. And that class is fully aware of it." In this respect, the struggle between capitalists and workers is a struggle over the degree of separation among workers.

Precisely because workers (given their needs as human beings) do resist reduced wages and increased work-days, capitalists must find a different way for capital to grow; they are forced to introduce machinery in order to increase productivity. By increasing productivity relative to the real wage, they lower necessary labor and increase the rate of exploitation. In the struggle between capital and labor, Marx argued, capitalists are driven to revolutionize the production process.

Marx traced in *Capital* the manner in which capitalists made historic changes to the mode of production in order to achieve their goals. Beginning with the pre-existing mode of production (one characterized by small-scale craftwork), capitalists used their control over production, their ability to subordinate workers, to extend and intensify the work-day. There are, however, inherent barriers against this method of expanding surplus value and capital, barriers imposed both by the physiological limits to the work-day and the resistance of workers. Accordingly, capitalists proceeded to introduce new divisions of labor, new forms of social cooperation under their control, in an altered production process. An important effect was to increase productivity and to nurture the growth of capital.

Nevertheless, even within this new form of manufacturing characterized by new divisions of labor within the workplace, there remained barriers to the growth of capital. This form of production remained dependent upon skilled workers, with their long periods of apprenticeship, and was subject to the resistance of those same skilled workers to the rule of capital within the workplace. Marx detailed, then, how by the middle of the nineteenth century capital had proceeded to grow beyond these barriers by altering the mode of production further – introducing machinery and the factory system. With this development of what Marx called "the specifically capitalist mode of production," capital subordinates workers not merely by its power to command within the workplace but by its real domination of workers in the form of machines. Rather than workers employing the means of production, the means of production employs workers.

Tracing the logic of capital well beyond the alterations in the mode of production that had occurred in his own lifetime, Marx described the emergence of large automated factories, organic combinations of machinery which perform all the intricate operations of production. In these "organs of the human brain, created by the human hand," all scientific knowledge and the products of the social brain appear as attributes of capital rather than of the collective workers; and, the workers employed within these "automatic factories" themselves appear as insignificant, stepping "to the side of the production process instead of being its chief actor."

The transformation of production through the incorporation of the products of the social brain, not surprisingly, generates the potential for enormous productivity increases. A good thing, obviously – it has the potential to eliminate poverty in the world, to make possible a substantially reduced work-day (one that can provide time for human development). Yet, remember, those are not the goals of the capitalist, and that is not why capital introduces these changes in the mode of production. Rather than a reduced work-day, what capital wants is reduced necessary labor; what it wants is to maximize surplus labor and the rate of exploitation.

Similarly, because it is not increased productivity but only increased profits that motivate capitalists, the particular technology and technique of production selected is not necessarily the most efficient; rather, given that workers have their own goals, the logic of capital points to the selection of techniques that will divide workers from one another and permit easier surveillance and monitoring of their performance. It is, of course, no concern of capital whether the technology chosen permits producers to find any pleasure and satisfaction in their work, or what happens to people who are displaced when new technology and new machines are introduced. If your skills are destroyed, if your job disappears, so be it. Capital gains, you lose. Marx's comment was that "within the capitalist system all methods for raising the social productivity of labor are put into effect at the cost of the individual worker."

There is another important aspect to the introduction of machinery. Every worker displaced by the substitution of machinery adds to what Marx described as the reserve army of labor. Not only does the existence of this body of unemployed workers permit capital to exert discipline within the workplace but it also keeps wages within limits consistent with profitable capitalist production. The constant replenishing of the reserve army ensures that even those workers who, by organizing and struggle, may "achieve a certain quantitative participation in the general growth of wealth" nevertheless would not succeed in keeping real wages rising as rapidly as productivity. The rate of exploitation, Marx believed, would continue to rise. Even with rising real wages, the "abyss between the life-situation of the worker and that of the capitalist would keep widening."

In short, Marx offers a picture in which capital has the upper hand in the sphere of production. Through its control of production and over the nature and direction of investment, it can increase the degree of exploitation of workers and expand the production of surplus value. While it may face opposition from workers, capital does drive beyond barriers to its growth in the sphere of production. Marx, however, noted that there was an inherent contradiction in capitalism in this respect: it cannot remain in the sphere of production but must return to the sphere of circulation and there sell its products as commodities – not in some abstract market but in one marked by the specific conditions of capitalist production.

THE SALES EFFORT AND "OVERPRODUCTION"

Insofar as capital succeeds in the sphere of production, it produces more and more commodities containing surplus value.

However, capitalists do not want these commodities. What they want is to *sell* those commodities and to make real the surplus value latent within them: they must re-enter the sphere of circulation (this time as sellers) to realize their potential profits. Here, Marx noted, they face a new barrier to their growth – the extent of the market. Accordingly, capitalists turn their attention to finding ways to transcend that barrier; just as they are driven to increase surplus value within the sphere of production, they are also driven to increase the size of market in order to realize that surplus value. Marx commented "just as capital has the tendency on the one side to create ever more surplus labour, so it has the complementary tendency to create more points of exchange." Whatever the size of market, capitalists are always attempting to expand it. Marx noted, indeed, that "the tendency to create the world market is directly given in the concept of capital itself. Every limit appears as a barrier to be overcome."

How, then, does capital expand the market? By propagating existing needs in a wider circle, by "the production of *new* needs" – the Sales Effort.[3] Once you understand the nature of capitalism, you can see why capital is necessarily driven to expand the sphere of circulation; it was only, however, in the twentieth century that the spread and development of the "specifically capitalist mode of production" made the sales effort so overwhelming. The enormous expenditures in modern capitalism upon advertising, the astronomical salaries offered to professional athletes whose presence can increase television viewing figures and thereby the advertising revenues which may be captured by media outlets – what else is this (and so much like it) but testimony to capital's successes in the sphere of production and its compulsion to succeed similarly in *selling* the commodities produced? For those commodities latently containing surplus value to make the "mortal leap" of sale successfully, capital must invest heavily in the sphere of circulation (which in a rational society would be grasped as an unacceptable waste of human and material resources).

Capital's problem in the sphere of circulation, however, is not simply that it must expand the sphere of circulation; it is that capital tends to expand the production of surplus value *beyond* its ability to realize that surplus value. Overproduction, Marx indicated, is "the fundamental contradiction of developed capital." There is a constant tendency toward overproduction of capital, a tendency to expand productive capacity more than the existing capitalist market will justify. Capitalist production takes place "without any consideration for the actual limits of the market or the needs backed by the ability to pay." Accordingly, there exists a "constant tension between the restricted dimensions of consumption on the capitalist basis, and a production that is constantly striving to overcome these immanent barriers."

For Marx, this inherent tendency of capital to produce more surplus value than it can realize flows directly from capital's successes in the sphere of production – in particular, its success in driving up the rate of exploitation. What capital does in the sphere of production comes back to haunt it in the sphere of circulation: by striving "to reduce the relation of this necessary labour to surplus labour to the minimum," capital simultaneously creates "barriers to the sphere of exchange, i.e. the possibility of realization – the realization of the value posited in the production process." Overproduction, Marx commented, arises precisely because the consumption of workers "does not grow correspondingly with the productivity of labour."

A period of huge increases in productivity while real wages lag behind is a recipe for overaccumulation of capital and its effects (as occurred in the Great Depression of the 1930s). How far are we from that now – with an enormous growth in productive capacity around the world in countries with low wages and a constant replenishing of the reserve army as peasants move (or are driven) from the countryside? The ability of capital to move to low wage countries in order to manufacture commodities that are exported back to the more developed world significantly increases the gap between productivity and real wages – i.e., it increases the rate of exploitation in the world, and it means that the sales effort to move commodities through the sphere of circulation must intensify. In this respect, there is more than just an obscene contrast between the low wages paid to women producing Nike shoes and the high endorsement fees paid to Michael Jordan and his like; there is an organic link.

The first sign of overaccumulation of capital is intensified competition among capitalists. (Why would that happen if the ability to produce surplus value were *not* outrunning the growth of the market?) However, the ultimate effect of overproduction is crisis, those "momentary, violent solutions for the existing contradictions, violent eruptions that re-establish the disturbed balance for the time being." Invento-ries of unsold commodities grow. However, if commodities cannot be sold under existing market conditions, they will not be produced under capitalism. So, production is reduced, lay-offs are announced – even though the potential to produce is there and people's needs are there. Capitalism is not, after all, in the business of charity.

In the crisis, the nature of capitalism is there for everyone to see: *profits – rather than the needs of people as socially developed human beings – determine the nature and extent of production within capitalism*. What other economic system can you imagine that could generate the simultaneous existence of unused resources, unemployed people, and people with unmet needs for what could be produced? What other economic system would allow people to starve in one part of the world while elsewhere there is an abundance of food and where the complaint is "too much food is being produced"?

THE REPRODUCTION OF CAPITAL

There's so much more to say about Marx's analysis of capital-ism – far more than any short introduction could hope to present. The increasing concentration of capital in the hands of a few large corporations, the division of the world into haves and have-nots, the use of the state by capital – all this can be found in Marx's examination of capitalism. So, too, can be found a profound grasp of the incompatibility between the logic of capital and Nature, between "the entire spirit of capitalist production, which is oriented towards the most immediate monetary profit" and the "permanent conditions of life required by the chain of human generations." Capitalist production, he commented, develops the social process of production "by simultaneously undermining the original sources of all wealth – the soil and the worker."[4]

Enough has been said, however, to grasp the essential story of capitalism that Marx painted – one in which the needs of capital stand opposed to the needs of human beings. It is a picture of an expanding system which tries to deny human beings the satisfaction of their needs but also constantly conjures up new, artificial needs to induce them to purchase commodities – a Leviathan which devours the working lives of human beings and Nature in pursuit of profits, which destroys the skills of people overnight and in the name of progress thwarts the worker's own need for development. So, why is this abomination still around?

It would be a big mistake to think that Marx believed that replacing capitalism would be an easy matter. True, capitalism was subject to periodic crises, but Marx was clear that these crises weren't permanent. He never thought that some day capitalism would just collapse. Nevertheless, in a crisis the nature of the system does come to the surface for all to see. Furthermore, it becomes more transparent with the growing concentration of capital. So, isn't that sufficient to lead rational people to want to do away with it and to replace it with a system without exploitation, one based upon human needs?

Marx did not think that there was anything so automatic about a movement to end capitalism. People might struggle against specific aspects of capitalism – they might struggle over the work-day, the level of wages and working conditions, over capital's destruction of the environment, etc. – but, unless they understand the nature of the system, they are struggling merely for a *nicer* capitalism, a capitalism with a human face. They are engaged merely, Marx stressed, "in a guerrilla war against the effects of the existing system" rather than in trying to abolish it.

In fact, nothing was clearer for Marx than the way capital maintains its hegemony, the way the rule of capital is reproduced. It continues to rule because people come to view capital as necessary, because it looks as if capital makes the major contribution to society, that without capital there would be no jobs, no income, no life. Every aspect of the social productivity of workers necessarily appears as the social productivity of *capital* – and, there is nothing accidental about this appearance. Marx commented that the transposition of "the social productivity of labour into the material attributes of capital is so firmly entrenched in people's minds that the advantages of machinery, the use of science, invention, etc. are *necessarily* conceived in this *alienated* form, so that all these things are deemed to be the *attributes of capital.*"

Why? At the core of all this mystification of capital, this *inherent* mystification, is that central characteristic of capitalism, that act wherein the worker surrenders their creative power to the capitalist for a mess of pottage – the sale of the worker's capacity to labor to the capitalist. When we observe that transaction, Marx noted, it never appears as if workers have received the equivalent of their necessary labor and have performed surplus labor for the capitalist over and above that. The contract doesn't say – this is the portion of the day necessary for you to maintain yourself at the existing standard. Rather, on the surface, it *necessarily* looks like workers sell a certain quantity of labor, their entire work-day, and get a wage which is (more or less) a fair return for their contribution – that they are paid, in short, for *all* the labor they perform. *How else could it possibly look?* In short, it necessarily appears as if the worker is not exploited – as if profits come from somewhere else.

Profits, it seems to follow, must come from the contribution of the capitalist. It's not only workers – the capitalist *also* makes a contribution and receives its equivalent. We all get what we (and our assets) deserve. (Some people just happen to make so much more of a contribution and so deserve that much more!) There you have the apologetic wisdom of the economists, who (as Marx noted) simply codify these appearances in elaborate formulas and equations. Nothing, though, is easier to understand than why this mystification occurs – given the form that the sale of labor-power necessarily takes on the surface. It is the source of "all the notions of justice held by both worker and capitalist, all the mystifications of the capitalist mode of production, all capitalism's illusions about freedom."

Furthermore, insofar as profits are deemed not to be the result of exploitation but to flow from the contribution of the capitalist, it necessarily follows that accumulated capital must not be the result of the workers' own product but, rather, comes from the capitalist's own sacrifice in abstaining from consuming all his profits – i.e., is the effect of "the self-chastisement of this modern penitent of Vishnu, the capitalist." Capital, in short, appears entirely independent of workers, appears as an independent source of wealth (all the more so, the more that science and social productivity appear in the form of fixed capital).

It cannot be surprising, then, if workers look upon capital as the goose that lays the golden eggs and conclude that meeting the needs of capital is simply common sense. By its very nature, capitalism generates the appearance that there is no alternative. As Marx indicated:

> The advance of capitalist production develops a working class which by education, tradition and habit looks upon the requirements of that mode as self-evident natural laws. The organization of the capitalist process of production, once it is fully developed, breaks down all resistance.[5]

It is this acceptance of capital that ensures the continuing reproduction of the system. Clearly, Marx did not think that replacing capitalism would be easy.

GOING BEYOND CAPITALISM

Nonetheless, Marx did think it was possible. Precisely because of the inherent mystification of capital, Marx wrote *Capital*, the culmination of his life's study. He believed it was essential to explain to workers the true nature of capital, important enough to "sacrifice my health, happiness and family." Marx, in short, wrote *Capital* as a political act, as part of his revolutionary project.

In order to understand what capital is, he stressed, you have to go beneath the surface and try to grasp the underlying hidden structure of the system. You can never understand capitalism by looking at the parts of the system separately and, focusing merely on competition, you will not understand the inner dynamics of the system: you will be lost in appearances, in the way the inner laws necessarily appear to the actors, and will not ask the right questions. Rather, you need to consider the system as a whole and to ask – how does this system reproduce itself? Where do the elements necessary for its reproduction come from? In short, where do the capitalists and wage-laborers necessary for capitalist relations of production come from?

What Marx demonstrated by examining capitalism as a reproducing system was that the capital that stands opposite the worker is not an unexplained premise (as it necessarily appears) but, rather, can be grasped as the result of previous exploitation, the result of previous extractions of surplus value. This same perspective of considering the system as one which must reproduce its own premises points to the shallowness of the view that wages reflect the contribution of workers to the production process. If workers are simply selling a quantity of labor and getting its equivalent, what ensures that they secure enough in return to be able to reproduce themselves? What, indeed, ensures that they don't (as a group) get enough to save up and *escape* from wage-labor? How does this system sustain itself?

By analyzing the system as a whole, Marx demystified the nature of capital. Enter into the logic of his analysis and you can no longer look at capital as this wondrous god providing us with sustenance in return for our periodic sacrifices. Rather, you understand capital as the product of working people, our own power turned against us. Marx's focus upon the whole, in short, illustrates that the point is not to reform this or that bad side of capitalism but, rather, the need to do away with the anti-human system that is capitalism.

This didn't mean that Marx attempted to discourage workers from struggling for reforms. On the contrary, he argued that not to struggle for themselves on a daily basis leaves workers "apathetic, thoughtless, more or less well-fed instruments of production." Marx's consistent theme was that of the importance of revolutionary practice, the simultaneous changing of circumstances and self-change. By struggling against capital to satisfy their needs, workers produce themselves in ways which prepare them for a new society; they come to recognize the need to understand the nature of the system and to understand that they *cannot* limit themselves to guerrilla wars against the effects of the existing system. That, as Marx knew, is the point when capitalism can no longer be sustained.

The society to which Marx looked as an alternative to capitalism was one in which the relation of production would be that of an association of free producers. Freely associated individuals would treat "their communal, social productivity as their social wealth," producing for the needs of all. They would produce themselves as members of a truly human community – one that permits the full development of human potential. In contrast to capitalist society "in which the worker exists to satisfy the need of the existing values for valorization" (i.e., as a means for the growth of capital), this would be "the inverse situation, in which objective wealth is there to satisfy the worker's own need for development."[6] In such a society, "the free development of each is the condition for the free development of all."

NOTES

1. I am very grateful to Doug Dowd and Sid Shniad for their comments on an earlier draft of this essay. I have taken many but not all of their suggestions.
2. I have chosen to use many direct quotations from Marx in this essay – not to send the reader in search of the source but to convey his point in language more compelling and relevant than mine. Most of the quotations from Marx are drawn from Volume I of *Capital* (New York: Vintage Books, 1977), the only volume of *Capital* that Marx completed, and from his rich notebooks of 1857–58 which have been published as the *Grundrisse* (New York: Vintage Books, 1973). I have used many of these quotations before (with proper citation) in my *Beyond Capital: Marx's Political Economy of the Working Class* (New York: St. Martin's Press, 1992), an expanded version of which is forthcoming from Palgrave Macmillan. See also for some of these arguments and quotations my "Marx's Falling Rate of Profit: A Dialectical View," in *Canadian Journal of Economics* (May 1976) and "Analytical Marxism and the Marxian Theory of Crisis," in *Cambridge Journal of Economics* (May 1994).
3. Marx himself did not use the term, "The Sales Effort." This was stressed by Paul Baran and Paul M. Sweezy in their *Monopoly Capital* (New York: Monthly Review Press, 1966), and I use the term to underline the continuity here between the latter work and that of Marx. The importance of "salesmanship" to twentieth-century capitalism was also a pointed theme of Thorstein Veblen.

4. For a good Marxist introduction to the problem of capitalism and the environment, see John Bellamy Foster, *The Vulnerable Planet* (New York: Monthly Review Press, 1999). A more detailed study of the centrality of ecology to Marx's view can be found in his *Marx's Ecology* (New York: Monthly Review Press, 2000). See also James O'Connor – both in his *Natural Causes: Essays in Ecological Marxism* (New York: Guilford, 1998) and in the journal, *Capitalism Nature Socialism* – and Paul Burkett, *Marx and Nature: A Red and Green Perspective* (New York: St. Martin's Press now Palgrave Macmillan, 1999).

5. Marx, *Capital*, Vol. I, p. 899. I break here from my pattern of not providing specific citations because, despite its significance, this passage (and others on the page) have not received sufficient attention.

6. Marx, *Capital*, Vol. I, p. 772.

2 THORSTEIN VEBLEN:
The Evolution of Capitalism from Economic and Political to Social Dominance; Economics as its Faithful Servant

Douglas Dowd

Thorstein Veblen's books and essays were written in the three to four decades preceding his death in 1929; in what ways, and with respect to which problems of our time can they be useful?

His stated focus was on economics and economies; in both areas, his analyses always reached out beyond the "purely economic" to combine with the sociopolitical, anthropological and psychological within an "evolutionary" framework – all of that grounded in his understanding of human nature and its dynamic relationships with the social process.

Veblen saw mainstream economics as mixing absurdity with obliviousness to the nature of both human beings and society; far from being the "social science" it purported to be, it was at best irrelevant, at worst ruinous, insofar as its precepts were taken seriously. Those "methodological" critiques will be discussed later, in the section entitled "Preconceptions vs. Realities."

Although his studies of economies focused mainly on the United States, he had much of importance to say about, and the differences among and between, the British, German, and Japanese developmental processes, and, as well, the nature of imperialism – what we today call "globalization." More specifically, the developments most commanding his attention were (1) the nature and evolution of the U.S. business system – its emerging giantism, its misuse of the new industrial technology, and its control of the then rapidly enlarging state; (2) the roots and consequences of imperialism and nationalism; (3) the emerging role of the media in the political economy; (4) the origins, nature, and meanings of what has come to be called "consumerism"; and (5) a persistent emphasis on the utter wastefulness associated with each and every one of these aspects of the social process: none of which, it may be added, gained any attention whatsoever from the mainstream economists of his day.

All those processes have been transformed and their damages spread and deepened since Veblen's time; if we are to understand and gain control over them his insights are thus more valuable now than when first put forth.

The ensuing examination of Veblen's works will begin with his general stance, proceed to his views on human nature, and go on to outline the key elements of his social analyses. Then, after a discussion of his critiques of mainstream economics, the chapter will conclude with suggestions as to the ways in which Veblen's analyses, when appropriately updated and integrated with others' contributions, can further our understanding of contemporary processes.

"DISTURBER OF THE INTELLECTUAL PEACE"

That phrase was used often by Veblen, and meant as a compliment. It was what he saw as the proper function of the intellectual. He lived up to it himself, not least in his general view that social existence has been dominated "by force and fraud," from the Egypt of the Pharoahs to modern democracies.

He argued that what becomes a "status quo" is constructed through force and *violence* and maintained by force and *fraud*, that the rule of "the leisure class" in its use of fraud as well as force is much assisted by its control over the technology of its time; and that not to submit to either the force or the fraud has always meant one form or another of peril to those so inclined: ridicule, ostracism, starvation, prison, a firing squad.

Veblen's main focus was upon the sources and uses of *power*, in the national or international political economy and the State, in organized religion, even in "the higher learning." Social power's ways and means vary from one sector to another, from time to time, and from place to place: but it rules, the force exercised through controlling "institutions," the fraud through an "institutionalized" socialization process – in the family, the schools, the workplace, the press, the church – in the culture.[1] Of course such views bore a strong connection to the realities of Veblen's time and place; but clearly something else was involved, something linked to his own "subjective" qualities. The latter cannot effectively be plumbed here, but the elements of his shaping objective circumstances can be.[2]

He was born to an immigrant Norwegian farm family in Wisconsin in 1857; by the time he was in his teens "the second industrial revolution" of physics, chemistry and mass production was well underway, as the "Gilded Age" and the "Great Barbecue" earned their names (from Mark Twain and Vernon Parrington). Whatever the benefits of those developments to some few, they were painful to workers and farmers – including the Veblens – who created the Populist movement of the late nineteenth century.

The uniquely spacious U.S. of Veblen was very different from the Little England of Marx – in its abundant resources, in its access to and uses of the new technologies, its giant businesses, its large population, and in the security of its physical isolation; but similar in that Marx's Britain and Veblen's U.S. were both dominated by capital and its industrial processes.

Veblen probably read more of Marx's and Marxists' works than anyone in the U.S. of his time. He admired Marx, but saw the need to expand his explanatory focus into the realms of sociology and psychology, to probe further than Marx as regards "what makes us tick." In doing so, he showed that we must understand the *culture* of what Marx called capitalism: Veblen called it "the pecuniary culture." It was more than a change of name, and it was that which he identified and analyzed in his first book *The Theory of the Leisure Class* (1899). The largest part of his subsequent writings (as often happens with great thinkers) may be seen as pursuing further and in greater detail matters merely touched upon in *Leisure Class*. Not least was that so as regards human nature.[3]

A glance at a few of the chapter headings of *Leisure Class* tells us what to expect: "Pecuniary Emulation; Conspicuous Leisure; Conspicuous Consumption; Pecuniary Canons of Taste; Industrial Exemption and Conservatism; The Higher Learning as an Expression of the Pecuniary Culture": all those "social" analyses are rife with tantalizing observations linking their functioning to the complex nature of our species.

His first major step in that direction was a short article in 1898, "The Instinct of Workmanship and the Irksomeness of Labor" (contained in IX). Adam Smith had used the term "irksome" to characterize "labor"; for Marx it was much more than that: "labor," in being exploited, was responsible for the "alienation," the dehumanization, of the working class.

Agreeing with Marx – though *never* using his vocabulary – Veblen's effort to show why "labor is irksome" launched him toward his considerably more substantial analyses that show how the historical process transformed work into labor, and, in doing so, suppressed the best and brought out the worst in us.

For both Marx and Veblen *labor* is a "dirty word," whereas *work* is not only life-saving but can be life-enhancing. In English we have allowed the two words to become interchangeable – even though our language derives mainly from Latin and German, where they have quite distinct meanings. In the ancient world, labor was the function of slaves, something done at the bidding of another to that other's gain; work, however arduous, is done at one's own "bidding," whether merely to survive or to fulfill oneself, or something in between. For Veblen, the "instinct" of *work*manship is what requires and brings out the best in us as a species.[4]

The further pursuit of those observations, and much more, came to be the substance of his *Instinct of Workmanship*, to which we now turn. Note first that Veblen uses the word "instinct," as with so many others, in his own way, to

> denote the *conscious* pursuit of an objective which the instinct in question makes worthwhile.... Men take thought, but the human spirit, that is to say the ... instinctive proclivities [decide] what they shall take thought of, and how and to what effect. (IV, pp. 5–6, emphasis added)

HUMAN NATURE AND CONDUCT

That was the title of a 1930 book by John Dewey, with whom Veblen had a mutually fruitful relationship. "Instinct," as used by Veblen, covers much of what Dewey referred to as "human nature and conduct" – most simply, our values, ingrained habits, feelings, tendencies and patterns of behavior, all shaped and affected by the social process, in a never-ending process of mutually transforming, cumulative, and irreversible change.

Used thus, Veblen saw us as living in accordance with two sets of conflicting "instincts," constructive and destructive. On our constructive side are the instinct of workmanship and its "partners," the parental bent and "idle curiosity." These are offset by a set of predatory and competitive "instincts," which Veblen in his ironic way bundles under the heading of "the instinct of sportsmanship."[5]

The instinct of workmanship "is in the main a propensity to work out the ends which the parental bent makes worthwhile" (IV, p. 48). And our "idle curiosity," the possession of which constitutes "man's great advantage over other species in the struggle for survival ..., [allows us] to turn the forces of [our] environment to account" (ibid.). Taken together, these lead us to cooperate among ourselves; they combine to preserve our species and to enhance our material and "immaterial" wellbeing.

It is our "idle curiosity" which, more than any other trait, sets us apart from the rest of the animal world; it refers to our ability and constant tendency to *imagine* and to *wonder*. It too has more than one side: that quality which leads us to hope, to dream, and to inquire also opens us to fears and foreboding and idolatry; that special quality in us which created music and astronomy created also racism and Hiroshima: without imagination, no Beethoven, but also no Hitler; the strengths creating literature are the other side of the flaws so well exploited and utilized by advertising and propaganda.

Our destructive other side has its distant origins in the essential role once played by hunting and killing; the continuous nourishing of that set of instincts has "contaminated" our constructive side, led us to become destructive of ourselves, of others of our species, and of nature – pushed always more fiercely by the powerful drives of capitalism and nationalism.

As Veblen is now quoted directly and at some length from his 1898 essay in what follows, understand that he uses "archaic" in reference to the "savage era" of hunting and gathering and that "barbarism" for him refers to the epoch that began with a settled agriculture and that endured and created our "pecuniary culture." Note also that those in "industry" are those who produce – workers – not, as we usually use the term, the businesses or businesmen of manufacturing, mining, etc., who own and control. The latter, as he puts it, are involved in "salesmanship," not "industry."

> Archaic man was necessarily a member of a group, and during this early stage, when industrial efficiency was still inconsiderable, no group could have survived except on the basis of a sense of solidarity strong enough to throw self-interest into the background. Self-interest, as an accepted guide of action, is possible only as the concomitant of a predatory life, and a predatory life is possible only after the use of tools has developed so far as to leave a large surplus of product over what is required for maintenance of the producers [i.e., peasants and workers]. Subsistence by predation implies something substantial to prey upon.
>
> ... With the increasing density of population that follows from a heightened industrial efficiency [settled agriculture, tool-making, etc.], the group passes ... from the archaic condition of poverty-stricken peace to a stage of predatory life. This fighting stage – the beginning of barbarism – may involve aggressive predation, or the group may simply be placed on the defensive.... When a group emerges into this predatory phase of its development, the employments which most occupy men's attention are employments that involve exploit.... The assertion of the strong hand, successful aggression, usually of a destructive character, becomes the accepted basis of repute.... Exploit becomes the conventional ground of invidious comparison between individuals, and repute comes to rest on prowess ..., the virtue *par excellence*, [and] gains in scope and consistency until prowess comes near being recognized as the sole virtue.... The honorable man must not only show capacity for

predatory exploit, but he must also avoid entanglement with the occupations that do not involve exploit. The tame employments, those that involve no obvious destruction of life and no spectacular coercion of refractory antagonisms, fall into disrepute and are relegated to those ... who are defective in predatory capacity; that is to say, those who are lacking in massiveness, agility, or ferocity.... In the further cultural development, when some wealth has been accumulated and the members of the community fall into a servile class on the one hand and a leisure class on the other, the tradition that labor is ignoble gains an added significance ..., not only a mark of inferior force, but ... also a perquisite of the poor. This is the situation today.... Labor is indecorous.

There is no remedy for this kind of irksomeness, short of a subversion of that cultural structure on which our canons of decency rest. (IX, pp. 87–96)

"The instinct of sportsmanship," as noted above, comprises our socialized inclinations to be predatory, competitive, and "invidious." In the millennia intervening between the archaic and our own era, force and fraud and habituation have allowed and caused those "instincts" to become dominant; but that's not all. As will be seen in the ensuing discussion of the *Theory of the Leisure Class*, a basic concept is that of "emulation." It is due to the strength of this tendency that "members of the servile class" (that is, the working class), instead of merely organizing in their own interest to create a different society, also, or instead, emulate those of higher income, status, or power.

The usual basis of self-respect is the respect accorded by one's neighbors. Only individuals with an aberrant temperament can in the long run retain their self-esteem in the face of the disesteem of their fellows. Apparent exceptions to the rule are met with, especially among people with strong religious convictions. But these apparent exceptions are scarcely real exceptions, since such persons commonly fall back on the putative approbation of some supernatural witness of their deeds. (I, p. 30)

It is this "emulative" tendency that sits at the center of the other major concepts of *The Leisure Class*: conspicuous consumption, conspicuous display, and conspicuous waste, to which we now turn.

THE PECUNIARY CULTURE AND THE LEISURE CLASS

Like so much of Veblen's terminology, his use of the term "leisure class" was unique to him; it requires more than a few words for its definition. He saw the leisure class – and "class" itself – as coming into existence in barbarian times, and as "institutionalized" in the feudal era. As Veblen uses his terms, we still live with the barbarian system, much transformed by the advance of technology over its millennia of existence, a transformation controlled, however, by a "leisure class" whose standards have endured, if in vastly different forms, from the savage era to the present. The members of the leisure class

> are by custom exempt from industrial [that is, productive] occupations, and are reserved for certain employments to which a degree of honor attaches ...; and this exemption is the economic expression of their superior rank. ... These non-industrial upper-class occupations may be roughly comprised under government, warfare, religous observances, and sports. (I, p. 5)

Seeing the leisure class as "guiding the growth of customs of habits and thought ... [especially] as it touches the institutions that are primarily of an economic character ...," Veblen goes on to distinguish "two classes ..., according as they serve one or the other of two divergent purposes of economic life." Marx's working class is Veblen's "servile class," or "underlying population."

Veblen's characterization of the leisure class is strikingly critical, and here put forth more forthrightly than usual:

> The relation of the leisure class to the economic process is a pecuniary relation, a relation of acquisition, not of production; of exploitation, not of serviceability.... Their office is of a parasitic

character, and their interest is to divert what substance they may to their own use, and to retain whatever is under their hand. The conventions of the business world have grown up under the selective surveillance of this principle of predation or parasitism. They are conventions of ownership; derivatives, more or less remote, of the ancient predatory culture ...; the immediate end of this pecuniary institutional structure ... is the greater facility of peaceable and orderly exploitation. (I, p. 209)

Observing in a footnote concerning business honesty and decency (II, p. 42) that "they will rather use wool than shoddy, at the same price," he also observes that

the characteristic attitude of the [leisure] class may be summed up in the maxim: "Whatever is, is right" whereas the [Darwinian] law of natural selection, as applied to human institutions, gives the axiom: "Whatever is, is wrong." (I, p. 141)

It is, of course, the leisure class that is "emulated." In noting that "the emergence of a leisure class coincides with the beginning of ownership," Veblen goes on to note – interestingly for one writing more than a century ago – that

the earliest form of ownership is an ownership of the women by the able-bodied men of the community, an ownership of the woman by the man [itself beginning] in the lower stages of culture, apparently by the seizure of female captives. (I, p. 19)

Moreover,

The outcome of emulation under the circumstances of a predatory life ... has been ... a form of marriage resting on coercion, and ... the custom of ownership. The two institutions are not distinguishable in the intial phase of their development; both arise from the desire of successful men to put their prowess in evidence by exhibiting some durable result of their exploits.... From the ownership of women the concept of ownership extends itself to include the products of their industry, and so there arises the owership of things as well as of persons. (I, p. 20)

From *Leisure Class* Veblen turned immediately to *The Theory of Business Enterprise* (1904). There he cast an eye both skeptical and caustic on the nature and functioning of business at home and abroad, and at their interacting economic and "non-economic" realms; and his emphasis was always on the use and misuse of power.

BUSINESS AS A SYSTEM OF POWER

This was the title of the 1943 book by Robert A. Brady, one of the U.S. economists most influenced by Veblen. Its focus was on the six leading industrial capitalist powers after World War I: Britain, the U.S., Germany, France, Italy and Japan. Brady traced out the same tendencies in all of them – toward an always increasing concentration and integration of economic, political and social power, which, in all but Britain and the U.S. produced fascism (obscured in France by the German occupation). In that book, as in other works of his, Brady (who had worked with Veblen) followed closely in Veblen's footseps and beyond, most especially as concerns Veblen's emphases on history, and the dynamics joining economic and "noneconomic" processes to socioeconomic power.[6]

The works on which Veblen focused most intently in the economic realm were *The Theory of Business Enterprise* (1904), and, amplifying and updating that, his last book, *Absentee Ownership and Business Enterprise in Recent Times* (1923). Both books took U.S. capitalism as their subject. Veblen saw its economy as becoming the most successful, most powerful, and most "rugged" of all capitalist nations – not just because of the benefits of its uniquely broad and deep resource base and the security from military attack given by its location, but also because it was the "purest" of capitalist societies: least constrained by the prior dynastic politics and inherited social traditions and controls marking the other leading powers.

At the center of Veblen's analysis was the ongoing interaction between the aims and methods of business enterprise and the logic of industrial technology. In his era, Veblen was unique among the economists in pursuing that set of relationships; he saw them as dominating the entire social process, and, most to the point, as being not only complementary and interdependent but, eventually, as conflicting and irreconcilable – a conclusion resting upon complex foundations, and requiring here at least a brief elaboration.

Those foundations brought together Veblen's views of the nature and diverse consequences of industrialism, of the interaction between human nature and the social process, and of the ends, means, and power of capital; his analyses of these and connected matters are found in four books: those just noted, and two discussed earlier: *Theory of the Leisure Class* and *The Instinct of Workmanship*.

At the center of his argument is his oft-stated epigram that "business is a means of making money; industry is a matter of making goods," and one of its by-products, "work that is, on the whole, useless or detrimental to the community at large may be as gainful to the businessman and to the workmen whom he employs as work that contributes substantially to the aggregate livelihood" (II, 63).

Implicit there, but explicit throughout his writings, is Veblen's conviction that U.S. industrial capitalism was simultaneously the most efficient and the most wasteful system in all history, and would become always more so in both respects. What may seem to be a contradiction is not: the efficiency is found in the productive techniques on the plant level; the waste is found in what is produced, how it is marketed, and its socioeconomic costs. It is worth noting that just as *Absentee Ownership* was published, the automobile industry, led by GM, took the first giant steps toward what has become consumerism, with its intertwined annual model change (which came to be called, by the industry, "planned obsolescence"), its massive advertising programs, and its financing of such purchases through consumer debt (by GM's new financial division, GMAC). Deliberate obsolescence soon spread to other durable goods production – including today, computer hard/software – and household indebtedness is 102 per cent of household income at the time of writing, as advertising in its manifold varieties (and disguises) has become the prime mover of popular culture – all this anticipated by Veblen in 1904 in *Business Enterprise*.

Veblen studied and understood modern industry and its technology considerably more fully than any economist of his time (as would be true, later, for Brady); his chapter on "The Technology of Physics and Chemistry" in *Absentee Ownership* remains instructive even today. His studies showed him the always increasing complexities of modern industry and, thus, the growing need for social control and planning. That need faced both the society and business, but the question arises, "control by whom? to what ends?" Like Marx – up to a point – Veblen saw the processes of industrialism as producing a working class tending toward becoming resistant to the ideology of capitalism, both because of their exploitation (a word he did not use) and because the "matter-of-fact" setting in which production takes place would be in conflict with capitalist ideology (and its seventeenth- and eighteenth-century roots). "Up to a point" because Veblen also gave much weight to what he saw as the tendency toward "emulation" by ordinary people – which is at the heart of consumerism's successes – of those who rule over them (in my view the major point of *Leisure Class*).

In this connection, it is important to note that consumerism in Marx's time not only did not but *could* not exist. However, just as Veblen's hopes for a workers' society were much tempered by his views on emulation and (as will be discussed shortly) other problems, so too Marx's expectations that workers would organize themselves to create a new noncapitalist workers' society should have been more tempered than it was by his own understanding of the dehumanizing effects of exploitation.[7]

In addition to the foregoing are the negative effects for workers' solidarity connected to imperialism, nationalism, patriotism and war. Marx, caught up in attempting to finish *Capital* (of which, he completed only the first of three volumes), merely noted such matters, but they were very much a part of Veblen's analysis of capitalist development, already in *Business Enterprise*, as well as in subsequent books – understandably, given that imperialism was already well-entrenched and producing intermittent "small" wars, with World War I edging over the horizon. All that, to say nothing of U.S. intervention in Cuba and the Philippines, provided ample evidence to Veblen that imperialism and bellicose propaganda were the other side of the coin of "business enterprise."

In *Business Enterprise*, Veblen combined the analyses of *Leisure Class* with the ideas that became part of *Instinct of Workmanship* and, especially, *The Nature of Peace* (1917). Patriotism and prowess are made the easier to promote by what Veblen saw as the "deep-seated inclination of man to display his prowess" – fitting nicely with business needs and opportunities:

Business interests urge an aggressive national policy and businessmen direct it. Such a policy is warlike as well as patriotic. The direct cultural value of a warlike business policy is unequivocal. It makes for a conservative animus on the part of the populace.... A military organization is a servile organization. Insubordination is the deadly sin. [And a bit later: The civilian population learns] to think in warlike terms of rank, authority, and subordination, and so grows progressively more patient of encroachments upon its civil rights.... At the same stroke [patriotic ideals] direct the popular interest to other, nobler, institutionally less hazardous matters than the unequal distribution of wealth or of creature comforts. (II, pp. 391–3)

Notwithstanding that Veblen foresaw in 1904 the likely triumph of business power over the threat of social change led by workers, he also saw it as likely to be a hollow triumph – in requiring the installation of an authoritarian and militaristic state; here the last paragraph of *Business Enterprise*:

It seems possible to say this much, that the full dominion of business enterprise is necessasrily a transitory dominion. It stands to lose in the end whether the one or the other of the two divergent cultural tendencies wins, because it is incompatible with the ascendancy of either. (II, p. 400)

Writing in 1915, Veblen anticipated both German and Japanese fascism (respectively in IV, and in IX, "The Opportunity of Japan"). Big business was a prime element in the emergence of fascism in both countries; however, not only did both countries lose a destructive war, but, well before that time, business in both countries found itself not ruling over but being ruled by the fascist functionaries – as exemplifed by the voluntary exile in 1938 of Hans Thyssen, head of Germany's largest steel company.

Just as Marx could not foresee what the early twentieth century would hold, neither could Veblen foresee the nature of its socioeconomy in its second half. What is remarkable in both writers is how very much of their analyses retains deep relevance – the emphasis of Marx upon alienation and exploitation and "the centralization of power" applies today to much more of the earth's surface and its peoples than in his own time; and the ways and means of business, and their shaping effects on human behavior and the social process are even more pronounced today than ever.

As Chapters 1 and 6 of this volume show for Marxian analysis, so it is for Veblen; their analyses can – and must – be adapted to current social processes and relationships; or, to put it more strongly, not only can our world be more easily understood with the assistance of their analyses; it may well be beyond our understanding without them.

If that seems an overstatement, it would seem much less so after a perusal of a large number of works in the realms of economics, history, political science and sociology which reflection shows could not have been done without the knowledge directly or indirectly obtained from Marx's and Veblen's works.

Veblen's many books and articles ranged over matters going well beyond what has been discussed here; although some of that will be touched upon in the summary section of this essay, it is left to the reader to pursue areas not discussed here.

Now we turn to economics, which, along with other inanities, assumes us all to be perfectly *rational* – that is, calculating, as distinct from *reasonable* – as workers, as consumers, and as capitalists. The discussion that follows is drawn mainly from Veblen's methodological essays, to be found in *The Place of Science in Modern Civilization* (1919).

PRECONCEPTIONS vs. REALITIES

What must we study if we are to understand the principal components – cultural, economic, political – of our social existence? And *how* must we study all that? Those are "methodological" questions. Then there is the question of the realities themselves, the whats, the whys and the wherefores of those "main elements." Veblen's life work was to answer both sets of questions, as much as one person might.

His methodological responses to the "what" and the "how" stood in sharp contrast with the senseless abstractions of the profession. He argued (1) that *economic* processes and relationships are central to our social existence, (2) that those processes are always *interacting* dynamically in mutually transforming relationships with our *sociocultural* lives, and (3) that all the foregoing must be studied as constantly *evolving* sets of processes and relationships, each "main element" affecting and being affected by the others, through "cumulative and irreversible causation."

Historical analyses thus become the necessary (though not the sufficient) condition for social understanding; with such analyses to work with, we are prepared to know what *questions* to ask of our present. The usefulness of scientific inquiry depends first and foremost on the questions it asks; and, as has been pointed out by Veblen (among others), the successful effort to answer each such question produces at least two more demanding study – and so on, *ad infinitum*.

Assume the evolutionary (that is, historical) approach is necessary; why give primacy to *economic* processes? Because, Veblen (and Marx) argued, throughout our history as a species, the time and efforts dominating our lives have been for survival; directly or indirectly, this "economic" factor has been primary in the shaping of our habits of thought and feeling and our ways of organizing our lives: our "institutions."

Thought of abstractly, much of the foregoing could be – but rarely is – agreed to by mainstream economists. However, the ways in which Veblen carried out those arguments in his many methodological essays and socioeconomic studies led him to a wholesale critique of the *status quo*: of nationalism, of *de facto* political oligarchy, of the business system, of the corrupted "higher learning," of "devout observances," and, underlying all of this, of the irrationality of our society. Unsurprisingly, he came to be seen as a heretic and a radical – or, more often than not, as a jokester.

Indeed he was all three. Heretic, because for Veblen nothing was sacred; radical because his historical analysis led him to locate the roots and attack the consequences of current "institutions" – whether "important," for example, as in the intrinsic role played by waste in the "pecuniary culture," or, seemingly "trivial," as with the determinants of women's fashions.

As for "jokester": In most of his writings Veblen was famously sardonic and witty, as well as convolute in his sentences – deliberately so, it seems, in order to soften or to camouflage the radical nature of his observations and conclusions. Understanding his society as well as he did, he inferred that the pill of serious social criticism will be swallowed only when it is coated with the sugar of humor: nicely exemplified by his earlier quoted characterization of the role played in neoclassical economics by its "hedonistic conception of man" and "timeless equilibria."

It may be added that if such "equilibria" are to be found in any science, it is the methodology of Newton, of physics – in which there is no need or room for anything approximating human history. But we live in irreversible time; if scientific metaphors and methods are to apply at all, they should have biology as the referent, with all its complexities and uncertainties, and all of its messiness.

More will be said about all the foregoing below (and in other essays of this book); but consider this for the moment. Veblen saw "institutions" as our ways of thinking, feeling, behaving, as the obvious and subtle ways in which we organize our lives, or have our lives organized for – or against – us; and as coming into being in order to resolve problems or to ease the way for new developments (for example, hospitals for illness, say, or the Internet for new ways); but he also saw that the intended functioning of such institutions *changed* the society, transforming existing problems and possibilities – and thus became "wrong."

Existing institutions are one way of describing "common sense" and "the status quo": what is, and what is accepted.[8] Veblen's analyses of his status quo made very *good* sense, but it had nothing of *common* sense about it.

THE APPLICABILITY OF VEBLEN'S ANALYSES FOR OUR TIME

In what must be a very short discussion, is it possible usefully to characterize the nature of "our time"? Here the attempt will be made, with the understanding that each element of that characterization should be taken as part of what is in effect a mere listing of the core elements providing the dire realities, dynamics and fearsome probabilities of this era. They take on different forms than in Veblen's time, of course; but it is a sign of Veblen's profundity that what we must deal with today was discerned by him when it was barely emerging. What are they?

In the social realm, what leaps to the front are the sources, uses, and consequences of widespread social *irrationality*. Veblen identified all those in his own time and anticipated their acceleration in the future. A reading today of *Leisure Class* and *Instinct of Workmanship* goes far toward informing us of the questions we must pursue today regarding "human nature and conduct"; as also, a thoughtful reading of *Business Enterprise*, *Absentee Ownership* and *The Nature of Peace* provides essential insights into the manner in which capitalist power has, can, and must function both domestically and globally to nourish irrationality if it is to slake its voracious appetites.

That irrationality, which Veblen saw as native to the very existence of a system of "business enterprise," quite naturally marks business behavior in all its aspects. Most obvious for us today are the relationships between business and the modern media, and their consequences. In Veblen's time that would have meant, almost entirely, print media; in our day they are included, but much more decisive are the combined effects of TV, radio, and film (plus the huge direct and indirect advertising of organized sports). In Veblen's day, the newspapers served the larger aims of business because they too were part of the business world and both capitalist and nationalist in outlook. Today the media are not only financed through business advertising but are increasingly owned directly by some of the largest corporations (of which General Electric, owner of NBC, among others, is the most obvious example).[9]

"Human nature and conduct" have changed much over the past century, but they have changed in keeping with Veblen's belief (as expressed in *Instinct*) that our nature is such that we are beset by two conflicting sets of "instincts" – constructive and destructive – and that what becomes of us and of our society depends upon which of those sets of instincts are most nourished by the ongoing social process.

Veblen saw our destructive side as being much strengthened in the time of our war with Cuba (which we called the "Spanish–American War"); but that was small potatoes when compared with, for example, the socialization processes accompanying the decades-long Cold War, a socialization process much enhanced by the consumerism it facilitated, and the powers of giant business to direct it. It is Veblen's reasoning as to the inherent importance of such powers and inclinations in our system that remain vital of understanding, still in our own time, if not more so.

However, to the degree that his reasoning was and remains valid, one element of it, that explored most fully in *Leisure Class*, commands our serious attention; that is, his emphasis on "pecuniary emulation." There he argued that the average person *not* of the "leisure class" is more likely to seek to be like those who are, than, as Marx had hoped and expected, to seek a society in which the leisure class would be eliminated, through the workers' creation of an economic, political, and social democracy.

Put differently, Veblen – and Gramsci, in his own way (see Chapter 3) – argued that it could never be enough for those who seek a different and better society to focus their efforts only on political economy; it was essential also to recognize the social and human constraints created and encouraged by capitalism, most especially to flourishing capitalism, a system whose success is measured in entirely quantitative terms having to do with the accumulation of capital and the commodification of everything and the suppression of other human needs and possibilities – at the same time as it allows, requires, and facilitates environmental disaster.

NOTES

1. In the essay by Carl Boggs that follows, it will be seen that Antonio Gramsci – a founder and leader of the Communist Party of Italy, imprisoned by the Fascists in 1926 until his death in 1937 – reached conclusions remarkably similar to, if also very different from, those of Veblen, most clearly in his concept of "the ideological hegemony of the bourgeoisie" and in his distinction between "common" and "good" sense. To my knowledge they did not know each other's works.

2. The definitive study of Veblen's life and times and their relationships to his work is Joseph Dorfman, *Thorstein Veblen and His America*. Published originally in 1934 by Viking Press, it is still available. See also the excellent book that focuses in upon Veblen himself, *Thorstein Veblen: Victorian Firebrand* (New York: M.E. Sharpe, 1999). All of Veblen's books have recently been republished by Transaction Publishers, as has a small book of mine, *Thorstein Veblen* (1964), whose aim it was to summarize and reorganize Veblen's principal arguments.

3. Of his many books, three may be seen as key to all his works: *The Theory of the Leisure Class* (1899), *The Theory of Business Enterprise* (1904) and *The Instinct of Workmanship* (1914). Citations from them will be identified for reference as I, II, and III, respectively. Others to be mentioned are his *Imperial Germany and the Industrial Revolution* (1915, IV), *An Inquiry into the Nature of Peace and the Terms of Its Perpetuation* (1917, V). *The Higher Learning in America: A Memorandum on the Conduct of Universities by Businessmen* (1918, VI), *The Place of Science in Modern Civilization* (1919, VII), *Absentee Ownership and Business Enterprise in Recent Times* (1923, VIII), and the fine book of essays edited by Leon Ardzrooni, *Essays in Our Changing Order* (1934, IX). Veblen's proposed subtitle for *The Higher Learning* was not permitted by the publishers; it was "A Study in Total Depravity."

4. In German the distinction is between *"arbeiten"* and *"werken,"* in Latin it is *"laborare"* vs. *"facere."* (On the arch over the entrance of Auschwitz is the infamous, mind-staggering sign *"Arbeit macht frei."*) Nor are these the only two words which in our time, alas, have lost their edge.

5. Veblen saw "sports" as being mostly highly competitive contact sports (boxing, football, etc.) or those "conspicuously displaying" one's access to leisure (fox hunting, lawn tennis, golf, etc.) – in either case, "invidious," at others' expense. Thus he noted that "It has been said that ... the relation of football to physical culture is much the same as that of the bull-fight to

agriculture," and pointed out that "the hunter proclaims his love of nature while setting out to destroy it."

6. *Business* ... was republished in 2001 by Transaction Publishers. The major "tendencies" of capitalism occupy the last third of the book; the earlier two-thirds concern the specifics for each of the six nations. Some may wonder at the inclusion of France as becoming "fascist." That France did not fully become fascist, it is generally understood, was prevented by its being occupied by the Germans. Brady was the most astute of U.S. students of fascism; his *Spirit and Structure of German Fascism* (1937) remains the best study in English of Nazi Germany, not least because it concerns itself as much with "spirit" as with "structure." That book was preceded by his excellent study *The Rationalization Movement in German Industry* (1933). It should be added that much though Brady was indebted to Veblen (and Marx), unlike Veblen, his meaning was never obscured by involute sentences, sly ironies, or a presumed neutrality; the difference between them may be seen as like that between a fox darting behind bushes and an onrushing bear. But Brady learned much from that fox.

7. This point has been thoroughly explored by Bertell Ollman, in his *Alienation: Marx's Conception of Man in Capitalist Society* (Cambridge: Cambridge University Press, 1976).

8. The foregoing has necessarily been all too brief. What is wrong with the form and content of mainstream economics, and alternatives to it, may be studied most beneficially in a recent book by Hugh Stretton, *Economics: A New Introduction* (Pluto, 1999). The book's strengths are numerous; among them is that as he examines each element of mainstream economics, from methodology through the various branches of analysis to economic policy, he also puts forth clear and workable alternatives. It is my view that anyone who takes the time to read it – and it is eminently readable – will, when finished, know more of what an economist should know than one with an economics degree from the best universities.

9. See the excellent book by Edward S. Herman and Robert McChesney, *The Global Media: The New Missionairies of Global Capitalism* (London: Cassell, 1997).

3   WHAT GRAMSCI MEANS TODAY

Carl Boggs

The prodigious theoretical, journalistic, and programmatic writings that Antonio Gramsci was able to complete before his prison-induced death in 1937, covering a span of barely two decades, amount to one of the most remarkable achievements in European intellectual history. Although the most extensive compilation of his works, the *Prison Notebooks*, did not reach a large audience even in Italy before the 1960s, and were scarcely known elsewhere before the early 1970s, they have become generally recognized – both within and outside the Marxist tradition – as one of the most powerful contributions to twentieth-century social thought, with an impact beyond Italy and Western Europe.

As with any other thinker, Gramsci's work can be seen as an expression of its particular time and place. In his preface to "The Study of Philosophy" in the *Notebooks*, he commented that

> Philosophy cannot be separated from the history of philosophy, nor can culture from the history of culture. In the most immediate and relevant sense, one cannot be a philosopher, by which I mean have a critical and coherent conception of the world, without having a consciousness of its historicity, of the phase of development which it represents ...[1]

This passage could just as well have applied to the evolution of Marxism in general, and to Gramsci's own theoretical influence in particular.

At the same time, Gramsci's thought has had an undeniably universal dimension, reflected not only in the continuing attention devoted to his work among intellectuals and political activists but in the great elasticity of his guiding concepts that still enjoy a definite currency. Gramsci's most important

contributions were his philosophy of praxis, his original concept
of ideological hegemony and his sensitivity to the all-important
phenomenon of mass consciousness, his theory of organic
intellectuals, his early attachment to the factory councils and
dual power, and his generally creative approach to the theme of
social transformation – all this constituted a novel vision of
democratic socialism even though, unfortunately, it was never
conceptually deepened in his largely fragmentary writings of the
1920s and 1930s.

Gramsci was above all a *political* thinker who saw in politics
a powerful lever of class struggle, cultural renewal, and community. He was the first Marxist to arrive at fresh concepts and
generalizations grounded in large-scale transformations that
were expected to occur within a rapidly changing capitalism –
and his insights turned out to be more prophetic than even he
might have imagined. The question I wish to address in this
essay is: precisely how useful are these concepts and generalizations for an understanding of contemporary post-Fordist capitalism? What dimensions of Gramscian Marxism remain valid as
we enter the twenty-first century? In other words: what does
Gramsci mean today?

THE GRAMSCIAN LEGACY

A persistent theme in Gramsci's Marxism was his effort to
merge the sphere of intellectual activity and political struggle –
that is to politicize or "democratize" theoretical work that in
earlier Marxism was divorced from what Gramsci called the
"popular element." For Gramsci, this uniting of theory and
practice, thought and action was not merely a guiding methodological principle but was also the driving spirit behind his
personal and political life. Revolution demanded not only
cognitive thought but passionate dedication and intense partisanship on the part of the theorist – a partisanship rooted in the
rhythm and flow of everyday life. Among leading Marxists only
Lenin devoted as much attention to matters of political *strategy*;
for both, the study of history, philosophy, and culture was
meaningful precisely as a guide to understanding the intricacies

of revolutionary action. And in the manner of Lenin, Gramsci was able to combine in a single personality the skills of political leadership and capacity for creative theorizing as few others were able to do.

Nonetheless, what distinguished Gramsci even further among Marxists (Lenin included) was his relatively humble social background (from rural Sardinia) and the close contact he maintained with working-class life and politics until his death only five days after being released from prison. The ethos of passionate engagement dominated every phase of Gramsci's intellectual output, as a passage from one of his prison letters to sister-in-law Tatiana Schucht revealed: "My entire intellectual formation was of a polemical nature, so that it is impossible for me to think 'disinterestedly' or to study for the sake of studying."[2]

To speak of an underlying continuity or thematic unity in Gramsci's thought does not imply a single, one-dimensional Gramsci whose entire range of contributions can be fitted into one mold. There was in Gramsci's Marxism three distinct but often crisscrossing paths – council democracy, Leninism, and Western Marxism – which do not correspond strictly to any chronological order.[3] In thus situating Gramsci, it is necessary to take into account the great variety of intellectual influences on his work both within and outside Marxism along with his deep involvement in a world defined by perpetual crisis, cataclysmic events, and unpredictable change. Gramsci's early commitment to the factory council movement – as a system of workplace democratic forms – in Turin represented a broad vision of revolutionary democracy he carried forward into his later writings. From the outset Gramsci wanted to understand the conditions under which a democratic shift toward socialism might be realized – the organizational forms, political tactics and strategy, leadership styles, role of theory, and view of the state. Gramsci's outlook here was rather distinct. Unlike other theorists and leaders of his time, he refused to equate democracy with prevailing liberal-capitalist institutions and practices or with Lenin's Jacobin conception, which imputed democratic content to the dictatorship of the proletariat associated with the Bolshevik party-state, insisting that socialism required novel forms of democratic participation.

What Gramsci had in mind, especially before the collapse of the *Biennio Rosso* workers' rebellions in 1920, was an organic process of social transformation that could prefigure the new communist society by gradually extending the domain of egalitarian, non-bureaucratic social authority and social relations into a mature socialist economic and political system.

There can be no question that Gramsci's main concepts in the *Notebooks* – "ideological hegemony," "social bloc," "war of position," "organic intellectuals" – were anchored to an unmistakable democratic outlook. He devoted much attention to reconciling familiar divisions within the Marxist tradition: party and class, intellectuals and masses, centralized leadership and democracy, and so forth. Indeed the very language of the *Notebooks* ("consent," "integrated culture," "organic," "ensemble of relations") demonstrates a sensitivity to the dangers of authoritarian politics, to what he sometimes referred to as "bureaucratic centralism." In addition, Gramsci's frequent allusions to a future "national-popular" movement in Italy were strategically tied to the idea of transforming civil society as a precondition of undercutting the division of labor in economic, cultural, and political life.

At the same time, with the failure of the council movement and the rise of fascism in Italy, Gramsci's earlier critique of concentrated power gave way to a more party-centered, or Leninist, outlook by the early 1920s. As a leading figure in the nascent Italian Communist Party (PCI), Gramsci endorsed the Comintern's binding principles (hierarchical command, tight discipline, closed membership, role of professional cadres) and looked to the vanguard party as flexible combat organization. Thus, from 1921 to 1926, deeply involved in PCI politics and immersed in the struggle against fascism, Gramsci's thought moved closer to the Lenin of *What is to Be Done?* He saw in the Comintern the only viable hope for preserving socialist identity in a crisis-ridden world. Gramsci's Jacobinism carried over into the *Notebooks*, especially in those sections of the "Modern Prince" where he invoked the legacy of Machiavelli as the "first Jacobin" who fully grasped the creative potential of politics. Here Lenin emerges as the contemporary parallel to Machiavelli – a bold, innovative thinker who celebrates the primacy of politics on behalf of unifying goals. The *Notebooks* were filled with references to the leading role of the revolutionary party, which for Gramsci embodied the universal interests of the working class and was indispensable for taking collective action beyond its parochial, spontaneous limits.

Still, if in his prison writings Gramsci set out to furnish a *theoretical* basis of Leninism, he also arrived at his own version of it. He was convinced that historical differences between Russia and the West called for entirely different political strategies: the notion of a dictatorship of the proletariat made little sense in Europe where the equilibrium between state and civil society was stronger than in less-developed societies.

Thus Gramsci's concepts of hegemony and war of position would lead to new ways of thinking about politics and the role of the party, introducing a language that was foreign to the Bolsheviks and to what later would be known as "Marxism-Leninism." The party Gramsci envisioned was less a combat apparatus geared mainly to seizure of state power than a "collective intellectual" or "myth prince" designed to carry out ideological functions as part of the war of position.

Gramsci's ideal party was conceived to do both, but its counterhegemonic role within civil society would take precedence during most phases of struggle. It might be argued that Gramsci's all-consuming aim in the *Notebooks* was to broaden, enrich, perhaps democratize Lenin's theory of revolution, rendering it more applicable to industrialized conditions of the West. Probably a more accurate view is that Gramsci found himself suspended between two conflicting tendencies – Leninism and revolutionary democracy – making it difficult for him to arrive at a non-Leninist resolution of the tension.[4]

The evolution of Gramsci's Western Marxist side is best understood in this context: with the paralysis of European Socialism and the collapse of revolutionary hopes after 1923, this theoretical shift was associated with a period of retreat and pessimism and, for Gramsci, the loss of his own freedom at the hands of Mussolini's jailers. Western Marxism involved large-scale efforts to reconstruct socialist theory along neo-Hegelian lines, returning to an emphasis on subjectivity, consciousness, and ideology that was missing from an orthodox Marxism still attached to objectivist views of economic crisis.

While immersed in PCI organizational life, Gramsci was naturally drawn toward immediate tactical priorities and the struggle for political survival, forcing his concerns in a largely instrumental direction. Once in prison, however, Gramsci began to explore his neo-Hegelian impulses for the first time; indeed the *Prison Notebooks* (notably the lengthy philosophical sections) stand today as one of the great contributions to Western Marxism. Gramsci's prison writings were directed toward understanding why socialism in general and the working class in particular had suffered defeat in the midst of mounting European crisis. He believed new historical circumstances demanded a full reworking of Marxism, but Gramsci was virtually alone in seizing this opportunity to formulate a new *political strategy* for the West.

If any single theme can be said to have shaped the *Notebooks*, it was the problem of *ideology*: hegemony, popular conscious-ness, culture, social bloc, the role of intellectuals were all dimensions of theory that revolved around this theme, as did his more instrumental focus on strategy. Surely Gramsci's famous concept of hegemony remains the most innovative and far-reaching construct in his body of work. Departing from Lenin's more narrow definition of hegemony as essentially ruling-class propaganda, Gramsci used it to explore the complex nature of bourgeois domination that he believed was manifest through popular "consensus" throughout civil society as much as through physical coercion by the state-military apparatus. Hegemony took on added meaning in advanced capitalism, where education, mass media, popular culture, and the legal system constituted pervasive ideological forces in support of the *status quo*, suggesting that the dictates of revolutionary strategy would have to change accordingly.

Here Gramsci theorized the prospects for an *alternative* hegemony – an emergent integrated culture – broad enough to delegitimate the existing power structure and lay the ideologi-cal groundwork for a transition to socialism. Consistent with the main premises of Western Marxism, this "war of position" schema contained two major implications: first, that the transformation of civil society takes place prior to and alongside the struggle for state power and, second, that the new state system must be built upon prefigurative, non-authoritarian foundations. Gramsci's insights into the state/ civil society relationship opened up new areas of theoretical inquiry within and beyond the Marxist tradition – a legacy that remains today.

Gramsci's full theoretical impact would thus not be felt until well after his death. Since he was a founder of Italian Communism, many observers – including many leaders and theorists of the PCI – later identified a "fourth tendency" in his thought: precursor of 1970s-style Eurocommunism. Any close examination of Gramsci's life and work, however, quickly reveals the falseness of this image. The fact is that none of Gramsci's main ideas can be said to anticipate the PCI's *via Italiana* strategy originated by Palmiro Togliatti in the 1940s and later refined by PCI elites in the 1960s and 1970s. In actuality, each of the currents in Gramsci's Marxism took shape precisely in opposition to the timid social-democratic politics which in the Italy of Gramsci's time most approximated what Eurocommunism later came to represent. Ironically, much of what Gramsci found anachronistic and debilitating in the old PSI (Italian Socialists) would be championed by the PCI in his name fifty years later: scientific Marxism, the parliamentary road to socialism, obsession with electoral politics, reformism confined to the existing Italian economy and state. Eurocommunist parties appropriated the stature and memory (but not the theory) of Gramsci in order to legitimate their political claims just as Soviet leaders used images of Marx and Lenin to justify their managerial rule.

Gramsci was convinced that the theoretical enterprise, much like politics itself, was filled with ambiguity, unevenness, and indeterminacy – qualities reflected in much of his own work. He never gave the impression of a theorist setting out to construct a closed system of thought based upon rigorous scientific principles, formal abstractions, or ironclad conclusive truths. What does emerge from a close reading of Gramsci, however, is one of the most original and compelling theories of the twentieth century, a body of thought embodying a rare synthesis of intellectual creativity, political refusal, and critical spirit – a synthesis pointing toward a renewed language of politics and contributing immensely to the revitalization of Marxist and critical thinking in the final decades of the twentieth century.

HEGEMONY AND COUNTERHEGEMONY

Gramsci's emphasis on philosophical discourses in the *Notebooks* grew out of a commitment that would later be integral to Western Marxism: to restore creative unity and dynamism to a Marxist tradition that by the 1920s had become deadened and conservative, lacking a transformative edge. This meant rediscovery of the critical side of Marxism with its emphasis on an indeterminate history, class consciousness, ideology, and above all for Gramsci, politics. The hybrid character of Gramsci's thought was an unsystematic but critical philosophy in which human knowledge was simultaneously a product of concrete historical forces and a *transforming* agent capable of remaking those same forces. Thus:

> To transform the external world, the general system of relations, is to potentiate oneself and to develop oneself ... For this reason one can say that man is essentially "political" since it is through the activity of transforming and consciously directing other men that man realized his "humanity" and "human nature".[5]

Gramsci called this the "philosophy of praxis," a crucial theme of which was the inseparability of consciousness (thought, feelings, will) and historical reality (the specific "ensemble of relations") – yet another way of stating the intimate relationship between philosophy and politics. Throughout the *Notebooks* we find repeated, in different ways, the notion that material forces acquire meaning only through human definition and engagement, that is, through a wide range of ideological mediations. This nexus philosophy–politics was not a submerged or implicit aspect of Gramsci's prison writings but a guiding thematic informing all his major concepts, above all that of hegemony.

The theory of hegemony, referring to processes of ideological and cultural domination that legitimate elite rule, is the analytical core that gives meaning to the continuous reflections on ideology, politics, culture, and consciousness in the *Notebooks*. It contains not only a powerful critique of mechanistic crisis theories favored by orthodox Marxists – for Gramsci there was no method for predicting the breakdown of capitalism – but also an implicit understanding of the system's capacity to reproduce itself in the face of material contradictions and social conflicts.

Theoretical insights into the problem of hegemony therefore suggested that historical change cannot be analyzed simply by looking at dysfunctions in the capitalist mode of production. In Gramsci's experience, attention to the ideological sphere grew out of historical events and political activity preceding his imprisonment as an enemy of the fascist state: collapse of social democracy, defeat of the council movement, the triumph of Mussolini. Yet, even as the *Notebooks* moved away from Gramsci's earlier triumphalism, the concept of hegemony in effect turned this pessimism around, adding a positive twist insofar as it broadened the view of capitalist dominaton and the means for overthrowing it.

Gramsci approvingly referred to Marx's dictum that people develop consciousness and become political actors in the ideological sphere, in support of the notion that consciousness itself is a decisive factor in the outcome of class conflict – not a mere epiphenomenon. Thus: "To the extent that ideologies are historically necessary they have a validity which is 'psychological'; they 'organize' human masses and create the terrain on which men move, acquire consciousness of their position, struggle, etc."[6] He saw that ideas, beliefs, cultural patterns, myths and even superstitions had a certain "material" reality of their own, since in their power to inspire people towards action they help *reshape* material conditions, which otherwise would exist as empty abstractions. From this viewpoint the contradictions of capitalism do not so much as "explode" as they are given cultural and political definition through human intervention. Here the concept of hegemony enabled Gramsci to view change in terms of the larger "ensemble of relations" that incorporated both material and ideological, objective and subjective elements of historical experience.

Gramsci approached this question from two separate angles. On one plane, he differentiated modes of control, distinguishing the functions of "domination" (physical coercion) from those of "hegemony" or "direction" (ideological power, consent) according to which bourgeois society has a "dual nature" exemplified by Machiavelli's Centaur, half-animal and half-human – "the levels of force and consent, authority and hegemony, violence and civilization ... ."[7] In dwelling upon the former, Marxists had virtually ignored the latter, with disastrous consequences for both theory and politics.

In calling attention to the consensual side of politics, Gramsci insisted that social orders cannot long be held together when relying mostly upon organized state power; what ultimately furnishes political durability is the scope of ideological consent or political support. The second aspect of hegemony centered around Gramsci's focus on insurgent movements as they struggle to build their own consensual legitimacy or counterhegemonic presence in both civil society and the state. To gain ascendancy, the working class would have to reach "hegemonic" status, going beyond the narrow "economic-corporate" phase of group, sectoral, or even class interests to the political or "universal" phase where a new moral–intellectual organizing principle for society as a whole could be established. The struggle for hegemony has two phases: to penetrate the false and irrational world of social appearances tied to the dominant order, and to create a new paradigm of beliefs, commitments, lifestyles, and social relations conducive to an emergent democratic socialism.

Gramsci's view of hegemony was therefore rather broad, extending to the whole field of ideology and culture that serves to mystify and solidify the prevailing class and power structures. Potential arenas of contestation are of course many: the state, legal system, workplace, schools, churches, the media, bureaucracies, even the family. Hegemony thus embraces more than discrete ideologies such as liberalism or nationalism. In advanced capitalism it might include not only the competitive individualism rooted in liberalism, but also the social atomization produced by bureaucracy, the fatalism instilled by religion, the state-worship fanned by patriotism, the fetishism of expertise resulting from technological rationality, and patriarchy endemic to the nuclear family. Gramsci argued that ruling elites always sought to justify their power, wealth, and status *ideologically*, with the aim of securing general popular acceptance of their position as something "natural," part of an eternal (therefore unchangeable) order of things. Gramsci observed that, insofar as these ruling ideas were internalized by the great mass of people, evolving into a defining motif of everyday life, they tend to appear as "common sense" – that is, as the "traditional popular conception of the world."

Hegemony performs certain functions that state bureaucracies, police, and military cannot, legitimating power relations and obscuring social problems while reinforcing attitudes of fatalism and passivity toward political action. Where hegemony succeeds in this way, subordinate groups can be induced to "consent" to their daily exploitations and misery. Such was exactly the situation Gramsci observed in Italy and throughout Europe, where capitalist elites held on to power in the midst of intensifying crises.

In posing the question of ideological domination, Gramsci never suggested that ruling-class adaptability was infinite or its power monolithic; on the contrary, he regarded the actual exercise of hegemony as problematic, the scope and intent of which needed to be investigated fully. Popular support for governing regimes varies from stable to precarious owing to availability of ideological "resources" to ruling elites, especially during moments of crisis. An example of fragile hegemony cited by Gramsci was nineteenth-century Germany where, as with the Italian Renaissance, intellectual and cultural life was restricted to a small nucleus of elites having little contact with the general population and thus unable to impose a clear "organizing principle" of their own. Not only the feudal aristocracy but the emergent bourgeoisie failed to establish the basis of national community. As in Italy and Russia during roughly the same period, regionalism and social cleavage prevailed over unifying tendencies and ideological consensus.

At the other end of the state/civil society equilibrium was France, where revolution burst upon the scene as a profoundly *mass* phenomenon – a national-popular transformation eventually giving rise to a durable political community. This development had its violent and authoritarian moments, to be sure, but once the convergence of elites and popular strata, city and countryside was achieved, the essence of a French unified nation-state was ultimately secured. Such a process never really occurred in modern Germany, or in Italy and Russia.

Given a sharpening crisis of hegemony and spread of counter-hegemonic tendencies within a given society, a crucial question must be posed: through what medium would local and dispersed struggles become unified and politicized? Gramsci believed the proliferation of social movements would reach a "cathartic" phase once established ways of thinking began to disintegrate, allowing for a massive crisis of authority and, ultimately, revolution. An organizational "solution" to the crisis would by itself surely be inadequate if oppositional movements and parties hoped to avoid an undistilled Leninist elitism. He paid great attention to ideological components of popular revolt, to "subjective" factors including symbols, myths, language, and traditions. The political response to new opportunities would have to be found in what Gramsci called a "revolutionary historical bloc", or "social bloc" – a convergence of counterhegemonic forces grounded in civil society but seeking expression on the terrain of state power. The term "bloc" adds conceptual refinement to Gramsci's rather vague treatment of mass consciousness in the *Notebooks*. He employed the notion frequently and in many versions, yet in each case it referred to historic crystallization of popular groups and movements built around a common ideology or social objectives, calling forth a collective sense of *political* identity going beyond the class dimension of public life.

Gramsci's definition thus went beyond strict material interests, or simple alliances, coalitions, and other loose configurations of social groupings, and it was not confined to the realm of state representation. "Bloc" usually involved a broad merging of forces, shifting and changing, at usually explosive historical junctures, leading to a process whereby "popular feelings became unified" and gave form to mass revolt.

The idea of durable social blocs was for Gramsci linked to particular strategic concerns: centrality of ideology, the role of nationalism, limits of parochialism, critique of economism, and the vision of a movement in Italy unifying the aspirations and interests of northern workers and southern peasants. Blocs furnish a concretely "global" dimension to local struggles that, if confined to partial spheres of activity, would eventually drift toward reformism or perhaps simply disintegrate. What this implied was a dynamic of popular mobilization around supra-class themes – nationalism, religion, anti-clericalism, regionalism, and so forth. The epic transformation of the PCI from tiny isolated underground organization into a dynamic mass party during World War II anti-fascist Resistance fits this pattern exactly, coming as it did with the worsening crisis of hegemony. Similar examples include the Spanish anti-fascist insurgency of 1936–39, the anti-Soviet Hungarian Revolution of 1956, new-left radicalism of the 1960s and 1970s around opposition to the Vietnam War, and growth of Polish Solidarity into a mass-based radical formation in 1980–81 made possible by the confluence of (anti-Soviet) nationalism and Catholicism. In each of these cases class relations were powerful but never decisive factors in the appearance of social blocs.

A focus on ideological hegemony and counterhegemony led Gramsci to explore the role of intellectuals relative to both their social position in capitalist society and their (potential) contribution to revolutionary politics. He was the first Marxist to take up the problem of intellectuals directly, as a *theoretical* concern, and it clearly informs the different phases of his thinking. But the term "intellectual" did not suggest for him *only* a particular kind of thinker or mental worker, or someone from the educated stratum, but also a general set of activities immersed in the moral–political aspect of class conflict. Intellectual *activity* would furnish cohesion and "homogeneity" to class formations and social blocs, serving to either reproduce or undermine ideological hegemony. Gramsci viewed ideological combat as increasingly salient to conditions of modernity, where the scope of hegemony expands in response to the growth of mass education, popular culture, the media, technology, and "Fordist" labor relations. In contrast to Russia, where the state was an isolated fortress surrounded by a hostile or indifferent population, in the West there was a narrowing of the gulf between state and civil society, between prevailing ideas and the "common sense" of the ordinary person. In the U.S., for example, hegemony had become more pervasive than in any other advanced capitalist society. Under such circumstances, where economic and political structures depended more heavily upon legitimating ideologies, intellectuals could be expected to assume a stronger role in politics, helping to link the social immediacy of class interests with global, unifying requirements of winning and exercising power.

Owing to these assumptions, the transformative power of Marxist theory could be actualized only through its critical, dialectical engagement with popular ideology, with the daily lives of working people, so that multiple layers of legitimation could be gradually exposed and subverted. Here Gramsci insisted that Marxism

> ... must be a criticism of "common sense", basing itself, however, on common sense in order to demonstrate that "everyone" is a philosopher and that it is not a question of introducing from scratch a scientific form of thought into everyone's individual life, but of renovating and making "critical" already existing activity.[8]

At the same time, the Marxist tradition was itself mired in the social division of labor: despite its well-known dedication to proletarian self-activity and egalitarian values, it replicated the divisions between intellectuals and masses endemic to class society in general. Marxism assimilated many characteristics of its social environment, since it too was deeply influenced by hegemonic norms such as elitism, professionalism, and individualism. Even Marxist intellectuals adopted an elitist culture, something found most frequently in Lenin and the Bolsheviks. Gramsci was preoccupied with resolving this impasse, with its far-reaching implications for socialist politics.

The seminal question Gramsci posed was: how, and to what extent, could the working class or social blocs generate their own (critical, oppositional) intellectual stratum? For a long-term solution he arrived at his now-famous theory of organic intellectuals, suggesting a "collective intellectual" enterprise with distinctly working-class features. "Theory" from this standpoint has no independent, contemplative status but would be integrated into the very fabric of everyday proletarian life, with intellectuals providing a bridge linking theory and practice, the organized and the spontaneous, the political and the social.

Gramsci understood that the bourgeois intelligentsia was the original source of Marxist thought, but argued that future social transformations should be governed by a more democratizing logic. Accordingly, the historical actor would be a "new type of intellectual" forged through the long process of class conflict itself, as part of the contest for hegemony. Thus:

> One of the most important characteristics of any group that is developing toward dominance is the struggle to assimilate and conquer "ideologically" the traditional intellectuals, but this assimilation and conquest is made quicker and more efficacious the more the group in question succeeds in simultaneously elaborating its own intellectuals.[9]

As the struggle for hegemony unfolds, oppositional (ideally for Gramsci, organic) intellectuals perform vital ideological functions: undermining myths that conceal class and power relations, putting forth critical views of the *status quo*, elaborating alternative visions of the future, and so forth. Yet such intellectuals were not likely to be either technical "experts" nor "learned men of culture" with their specialized, esoteric discourses far removed from daily life; "organicity" meant nothing less than immersion in all spheres of proletarian existence.

This idea suggested thorough reformulation of the way intellectual activity had been conceived both within and outside Marxism. "Directive," organizing functions remained central but, to be effective, they would have to be grounded in the working-class milieu of factories, offices, cafes, community life, and everyday culture, with the aim of overcoming the historic gulf between intellectuals and masses that was integral to class society (and in Italy, Catholicism).

With the Turin council movement always in mind, Gramsci saw organic intellectuals as a democratizing force inseparable from the life of the average worker, yet capable of moving the great mass of people toward revolution. In this spirit Gramsci referred to theory as a "popular" enterprise and championed the radical notion that all human beings must be regarded as in some sense intellectuals insofar as they carry out various mental activities, enter into social relations, express opinions, and make endless choices regarding their lives. This subversive view would have dramatic repercussions, since "... a new way of conceiving the world and man is born and this conception is no longer reserved to the great intellectuals, to professional philosophers, but tends to become a popular, 'mass' phenomenon."

Yet if Gramsci's Marxism had little in common with the notion of "scientific" theory elaborated by learned intellectuals – a view favored by both Kautsky and Lenin – it would nonetheless require some element of political specificity and cohesion. In certain respects the factory councils, more or less collective and democratic in form, radical and localist in ideology, seemed to be the perfect setting for the appearance of organic intellectuals on a large scale. When, however, the councils were destroyed or neutralized in postwar Europe, disillusioned leftists gravitated toward the vanguard party which, after all, had managed to conquer power and establish a new state in Russia. This was particularly true in Italy.

After 1921, therefore, it was hardly surprising to find Gramsci attracted to the idea of a highly-organized party as "myth prince" – a semi-Leninist theme figuring strongly in the *Prison Notebooks.* Gramsci's anti-elitism therefore soon gave way to historical pressures: he now concluded that the Communist Party should become the repository of theory, its leadership the final arbiter of political strategy.

Yet Gramsci's understanding of the vanguard party, as with his view of intellectuals, departed from Lenin's in many ways, starting with his emphasis on the ideological role of the party consistent with the "war of position" schema directed first toward transforming civil society. Gramsci had serious problems with the strict Leninist boundaries established between the political and social realms exemplified by the notion of professional cadre, which became the hallmark of later Bolshevik parties.

In the end, however, Gramsci never completely escaped the Leninist vanguardism that permeated his thinking in circumstances where historical pressures seemed overpowering. His fascination with Machiavelli and Lenin was hardly tangential to his perspectives on methods and strategy. The dilemma he so brilliantly set forth – whether, and in what ways, the proletariat might develop its own counterhegemonic intellectuals – was thus never resolved. Among other problems, Gramsci failed to identify the actual *source* of organic intellectuals. They were not likely to emerge from the working class itself, since its subordination to dominant world views served to block emergence of a "collective intellectual" stratum needed to carry out social transformation; in the absence of mediations ordinary people were not likely to transcend the parameters of "common sense." At the same time, to have located the source within the bourgeois intelligentsia would be self-defeating, starkly at odds with Gramsci's general view of a mass-based democratic project.

Left with this ambiguity – that is, without any real historical agency – Gramsci ultimately reverted to the vanguard party, meaning that intellectuals would be "organic" largely within a centralized organization designed to turn them into *political* intellectuals. Such tensions and contradictions resonated throughout Gramsci's work.

FORDISM AS CAPITALIST HEGEMONY

At the other extreme from societies marked by weak equilibrium between state and civil society, far removed from Germany, Italy, and Russia, Gramsci looked to the United States as a country where the ruling class had established the most complete hegemony. Like other European Marxists, he believed that the unique success of American capitalism – and the concomitant weakness of socialism – could be explained by the absence of feudalism and, as it turned out, he was able to connect this historical fact to his broader theory of hegemony. Gramsci wrote that the first Anglo-Saxon pioneers settling America brought with them a new "moral energy," a "new level of civilization" untrammeled by preindustrial residues that made possible a virtually limitless expansion of capitalism. With no feudal restraints, obstacles to capitalist development (and later corporate domination) were more readily overcome in the U.S. than in more tradition-bound European nations. As Gramsci put it, the absence of parasitic sedimentations left behind by past phases of history had allowed industry, and commerce in particular, to advance on a comparatively sound basis.

The key element of American politics was that the life of the country had always revolved around the capitalist economy, from which emerged a new type of human being, a new work process, a new dynamic materialist culture with no feudal survivals (monarchy, nobility, peasantry) and, as a corollary to all this, a poorly-developed political opposition in comparison with most European societies. Gramsci added that the very mode of social existence found in liberal capitalism paved the way toward the later success of bureaucratic–corporate forms of rationality; indeed the phenomenon Gramsci labeled "Fordism" or "Americanism" seemed to apply to both liberalism and technological rationality – or at least their convergence took on a "natural" veneer in a setting where bourgeois hegemony met with so little resistance.

By the 1920s American enterprises, with Henry Ford leading the way, became the "prototype of the new industrialism" made possible by innovative forms of machine technology and bureaucratic control over the labor force. The natural ideological expression of this process – technological rationality – was now assimilated into the complex forms of ideological and cultural control. Here Gramsci saw in the process of rationalization the leading edge of a new epoch: the ruling classes were no longer just obsessed with efficiency and profits but were anxious to stave off economic crisis and reconsolidate the system on firmer ideological ground. Hence "Fordism" represented "the passage from the old economic individualism to the planned economy." [10]

As the linchpin of a Fordist organized and planned economy, bureaucracy and technology were not simply fixed ingredients of an industrialization process; they were part of a larger system of *domination*, and the rationality they embodied would become a hegemonic force of significant proportions – not just in the U.S., of course, but throughout the developed capitalist economies.

In the *Notebooks* Gramsci paid considerable attention to the destructive effects that new industrial techniques – notably "scientific management," or Taylorism – had upon working-class life. Gramsci was probably the first Marxist to anticipate the massive consequences of rationalization for capitalist development as a whole: transition to a bureaucratically-integrated state, appearance of new forms of social control, the degradation of work, the blunting of proletarian consciousness. His opportunity to reflect upon the Italian fascist experience of the 1920s and 1930s no doubt contributed to this theoretical foresight. Whether in the guise of Fordism or corporatism, the liberal state or fascist dictatorship, Gramsci viewed rationalization as everywhere subversive of intellectual, political, and workplace creativity within the labor process – a tendency seemingly at odds with his vision of counterhegemonic movements arising out of the very infrastructure of capitalist industry.

The new instrumentalism and secular "theology" of technological rationality emanating from the Fordist system would impose ever more rigid barriers to oppositional politics. The rationalization of production and work, most advanced in the U.S., required a "collective man" or "mass worker" who could passively carry out routine tasks and unthinkingly conform to a suffocating labor discipline. By reducing workers to obedient automatons, rationalization would break down the very capacity to resist exploitation and organize for change. Gramsci saw in Henry Ford an innovative corporate general who perceived the immense productivity and control benefits to be derived from regulating every aspect of the worker's life. The ultimate goal was to create a routinized psychic structure compatible with the imperatives of machine technology and strict labor discipline. To this end Fordism, moved along by its own logic, embraced an unprecedented regulation of both work and "private" life; indeed, rationalization seemed bound to obliterate the public/personal distinction beyond even what Puritanism desired.

Gramsci saw in this coerced fusion of public and personal life a dangerous trend toward a fully-regulated society where Fordism might become a type of "state ideology." This was in fact the trajectory of European fascism during Gramsci's own lifetime. The American mode, in contrast to Mussolini's vision of a corporate state, was not likely to fulfill such Orwellian projections: *state* control of social and personal life never approached fascist levels, while Puritanism and sexual oppression in fact subsequently *declined* with further industrialization. Gramsci vastly exaggerated capitalist requirements for the stable monogamous sexual relations he assumed were integral to Fordism. From the standpoint of the connection between rationalization and hegemony, however, Gramsci's prescient understanding of "Americanism" was well ahead of its time. More significantly, his view of technological rationality as a powerful element in shaping mass consciousness was a theoretical departure not only within Marxism but also within the broader reaches of European social theory. The sketchy notes assembled in "Americanism and Fordism" might therefore be viewed as a preliminary statement to later work on rationalization by Theodore Adorno and Max Horkheimer (*Dialectic of Enlightenment*), Herbert Marcuse (*One Dimensional Man*), and Harry Braverman (*Labor and Monopoly Capital*) among others.

If Gramsci's argument that capitalist rationalization would give rise to a depoliticized mass consciousness was valid, then the familiar Marxist expectation of mounting class strife with higher levels of industrialization becomes problematic: the system could now stabilize itself in the face of even the most intense economic crises. Here Gramsci's commentary in "Americanism and Fordism" can be read as a theoretical concession to the traumatic *political* defeats suffered by the European working class in the early 1920s. At this point Gramsci may well have been resigned to a lengthy phase of capitalist reconsolidation made possible by modern technocratic engineering. Surely he bemoaned the decline of the type of skilled and rebellious workers who formed the nucleus of the Turin factory council movement. What the spread of a routinized proletarian existence signaled more than anything was the irretrievable erosion of class autonomy relative to capital, and hence the weakening of struggles for self-management.

Gramsci's analysis of rationalization, however fragmentary and tentative, shared more in common with Marx's theory of the fetishism of commodities and Lukacs' concept of reification than his general, more dialectical views of hegemony and counterhegemony would suggest.

Pushed to its extreme, such a perspective winds up suppressing that side of Marxism oriented toward proletarian self-activity – a side, moreover, closest to Gramsci's own philosophy of praxis and his earlier focus on the "actuality of the revolution." Where rationalization allows the system to regenerate itself, agencies of resistance and transformation are enfeebled; the dynamics of class struggle are undercut in the face of strengthening bourgeois hegemony. For if workers are indeed reduced to "trained gorillas" – that is, are made into atomized and degraded objects – by the new production regimen, then the very psychological basis of proletarian subjectivity is negated. Of course this was not the precise conceptual framework Gramsci wanted to construct. But he did set out to grasp the central features of an entirely new phase of capitalist development in the West – an organized and planned (state) capitalism just beginning to engulf most areas of social life. Despite lapsing into a certain one-dimensionality here, Gramsci did perceptively identify the main barriers to political opposition erected by a rationalized state economy. At the same time, this system would presumably become the source of new and explosive contradictions of its own, giving rise to a refocused dialectic of change that Gramsci barely glimpsed and thus could not have theoretically elaborated during his prison years.

Gramsci's more general views on philosophy and politics did suggest the future appearance of countervailing tendencies to rationalized domination; beneath a nearly totalitarian surface workers (both unskilled and skilled) would eventually be driven to resist. Since routinization of production could never fully obliterate local autonomy and creativity, even American industrialists

> have understood that "trained gorilla" is just a phrase, that "unfortunately" the worker remains a man and even that during his work he thinks more ... once he has overcome the crisis of adaptation without being eliminated: and not only does the worker think, but the fact that he gets no immediate satisfaction from his work and realizes that they are trying to reduce him to a trained

gorilla, *can lead him into a train of thought that is far from conformist.*[11]

When viewed as part of Gramsci's overall theory, then, the schema outlined in "Americanism and Fordism" actually pointed to a new phase of class struggle and, equally significant, to a new arena in which it would be waged, although its full implications were never spelled out in the *Notebooks*. The new arena was that of ideological combat within the process of capitalist rationalization, intensified by the growth of new educational, technological, cultural, and intellectual forces within civil society. In fact the development of an increasingly complex "ensemble of relations" in advanced capitalism – parties and trade unions, a large technical and managerial stratum, mass education and popular media, the deepening penetration of civil society by the state – would endow the struggle for ideological hegemony an immediacy it did not have previously.

A GRAMSCIAN STRATEGY?

The appearance of local popular movements in many societies since the 1960s does not in itself necessarily generate any cohesive or unified, much less counterhegemonic political opposition; it can, and often does, lead to something altogether different – a splintering of social forces, movements, and interests that has more recently become associated with post-modernism and identity politics. This shift, visible throughout the industrialized world, derives its energy from a sense of difference, plurality, locale, and multiculturalism – a trans-formative outlook where it involves a breakdown of old cultural barriers and widening of the public sphere, but problematic where discourses of fragmentation, insularity, and "local knowl-edge" deflect attention away from the broader concerns of institutional change and political strategy, which were always preeminently Gramscian concerns. In a social order where the symbols and images of a corporate-driven media culture perme-ate mass consciousness, the splintering of local identities coincides with the decline of political opposition. Corporate power winds up only feebly challenged by the scattering of movements which, in the absence of a cohesive social bloc, become easily assimilated into the all-powerful commodity. Identities end up detached from the public sphere while politics descends into an endless cycle of charades and spectacles.[12] Where this holds true, the deeper significance of critical intellectuals in the post-Fordist setting is generally diminished. The famous postmodern turn is thus overcome by dilemmas: turbulence, conflict, and sharpened antagonisms do not logically point toward any specific mode of social change or political representation.

Here Gramsci's concept of social bloc is once again suggestive, both as critique of postmodern chaos and as outline of counterhegemonic politics in post-Fordist society. Where dispersed identities, constituencies, and movements run up against the imperatives of viable political action, the development of a social bloc in Gramscian terms implies a transcendence of this impasse: a coalescing of local struggles into a strong political opposition injecting into the "war of position" a definite ideological meaning. Trends in the U.S. since the 1970s have worked in just the opposite direction, hastened along by the weakening of left politics that comes with the general depoliticization of society. Gramsci, as we have seen, looked to critical historical rallying points as the source of unifying popular mobilization. Viewed globally, in the postwar years only the New Left and Polish Solidarity would appear to fit Gramsci's understanding of social bloc although both deteriorated once the unifying historical events (Vietnam War, Soviet domination of Poland) lost their resonance. In recent times the main glimmer on the horizon has been a series of well-planned grassroots struggles against corporate-driven globalization – first visible during the Seattle protests of late 1999 – that brought together representations of labor, community groups, NGOs, and new social movements. The advantage of this phenomenon is that globalization through its very logic has *universal* consequences, its destructive impact certain to be magnified in the future. As a focal point of popular mobilization, however, the issue may be too remote from people's daily lives (or at least will be perceived

as such) to sustain the needed psychological and social immediacy which, as Gramsci observed, is the *sine qua non* of bloc
formation. We also know that movement linkages within the
anti-globalization campaigns have generally been tenuous and
fragile, a limitation sharpened by the absence of any counterhegemonic *ideology*.

Owing to historical pressures and the fragmentary, tentative
character of his work Gramsci's legacy must be viewed as a
strongly divided one, a fact made all the more salient by the
long-term erosion of Marxism itself as a source of analysis and
political strategy. Yet Gramsci's rich and complex body of
writings, especially the part belonging to Western Marxism,
does suggest the outlines of a democratic-socialist transformation that, under more propitious circumstances, could help
shape an oppositional politics. The work points toward a
strategic model combining radical insurgency and democratic
forms tied to the simultaneous transformation of civil society
and the state system. That Gramsci's opus remains so widely
respected and influential among new generations of intellectuals, many decades after his death, testifies to the great elasticity,
perhaps even universality, of the concepts he formulated. Taken
together, these seminal concepts were, during Gramsci's life at
least, inspired by a profound sense of political optimism
("actuality of the revolution") along with a commitment to
democratic ideals and practices. The unfortunate ideological
limits to such thinking today should not, of course, be laid at
Gramsci's doorstep.

We can see more clearly with historical hindsight just how
partial and uneven was Gramsci's critique of Fordist rationalization, just as we can better appreciate internal flaws at work
within the entire Marxist tradition. Gramsci focused his analysis mainly on the factory, on the emergent Fordist workplace,
assuming that modernity could simply be turned around
through the inexorable unfolding of proletarian emancipation –
a Marxist variant of Enlightenment rationality. Gramsci was
surely insightful about the crippling effects of capitalist rationalization but he never drew conclusions from this regarding the
immense ideological obstacles it would place in the way of
social transformation. Attached to the idea of socialism as a

radical extension of modernity, he had no critique of industrial society that went beyond the factory-based system of exploitation and, as we have seen, his view of rationalization never incorporated those global hegemonic influences that later became so decisive: expansion of commodity culture, consumerism, technological rationality, and the mass media. But a reconstituted Gramscian outlook does allow for, indeed strongly encourages, theoretical discourses that move along such a path, quite an astonishing legacy for a thinker whose most important writings were furtively scribbled during many painful years in fascist prisons.

NOTES

1. "The Study of Philosophy", in Quintin Hoare and Geoffrey Nowell Smith, eds, *Selections from the Prison Notebooks of Antonio Gramsci* (*SPN*) (London: Lawrence and Wishart, 1971), p. 324.
2. "Letter to Tatiana", December 15, 1930, in Lynne Lawner, ed., *Antonio Gramsci: Letters from Prison* (New York: Harper and Row, 1973), p. 193.
3. For a more elaborate discussion of the "three faces" of Gramsci, see Carl Boggs, *The Two Revolutions: Gramsci and the Dilemmas of Western Marxism* (Boston: South End Press, 1984), ch. 1.
4. Boggs, *The Two Revolutions*, pp. 267–8.
5. "The Study of Philosophy", *SPN*, p. 360.
6. "The Study of Philosophy", *SPN*, p. 377.
7. "The Modern Prince", *SPN*, pp. 169–70.
8. "The Study of Philosophy", *SPN*, pp. 330–1.
9. "The Intellectuals", *SPN*, p. 10.
10. "Americanism and Fordism", *SPN*, p. 279.
11. "Americanism and Fordism", *SPN*, p. 304.
12. On the process of depoliticization in post-Fordist society, see Carl Boggs, *The End of Politics: Corporate Power and the Decline of the Public Sphere* (New York: Guilford, 2000), ch. 1.

4 CRITICAL INSTITUTIONALISM: From American Exceptionalism to International Relevance

Michael Keaney

Critical institutionalist economics encompasses a large swathe of non-neoclassical economic inquiry. Rejecting mainstream ideas of equilibrium and constrained optimization together with its static modeling methodology, institutionalists instead emphasize the importance of history, culture and geography to the study of economic problems. The very definition of these problems they view as fundamentally different from the questions posed by neoclassical economists. Recognizing change as a given in human existence, institutionalists have incorporated and adapted the insights of Charles Darwin in order to develop a more relevant basis for the formulation of theory and conduct of analysis. In large measure critical institutionalism owes its uniqueness to the legacy of Thorstein Veblen, whose work continues to inform the development of institutionalist theory and analysis today.

It has become fashionable in recent years for economists and political scientists to affirm the importance of social institutions. There has grown a "new institutionalism" which has spawned numerous research projects among academics, in so doing providing the framework for subsequent discussion of institutional problems. Critical institutionalism has been relegated to the status of old by those who believe that economics has progressed as a science. However, as William Dugger points out:

> The so-called "new institutionalism" is critical neither of the existing economic system nor of dominant economic theory. However, the so-called "old institutionalism" is critical of both. Hence, all we need to do is call "old" institutionalism critical institutional-

ism and call "new" institutionalism noncritical institutionalism. Doing so gives us unambiguous labels that refer to real characteristics of the school being labeled. Doing so also removes the inappropriate stigma from our school of being old – probably outdated and stagnant – and removes the inappropriate, positive aura from their school of being new – probably updated and improved.

The difference between noncritical or neoclassical institutionalism and its critical counterpart can be readily highlighted. Douglass C. North, a pioneer of "new" institutionalism, was awarded the "Nobel" prize in economics in 1993 in recognition of his contributions to the discipline. One such contribution was his statement in 1978 that "to abandon neoclassical theory is to abandon economics as a science." By the time he received his award he could acknowledge that neoclassical theory could not account for the poor economic performance of less developed countries. According to North, what was required instead was a focus upon institutions, which "provide the key constraints and therefore shape incentives." To what end? "A necessary condition for efficient markets which underlie high income societies are channels of exchange, both political and economic, which make possible credible agreements." In other words, North is arguing that merely assuming the existence of "efficient markets," implicit in neoclassical economics, is insufficient. What is required is an understanding of the institutions that impede progress toward the end of market efficiency, and the means thereby of its attainment. The traditional neoclassical assumption that market exchange is costless meant that institutions could be ignored. However, once the costs of market transactions are recognized, so too is the importance of institutions, inasmuch as these facilitate or impede exchange. Thus, in defining institutional efficiency as the minimization of transaction costs, the "new institutionalists" are simply applying neoclassical theoretical principles to another aspect of social life. Unaltered is the notion of human beings as independent, rational utility-maximizers. Another of the main originators of the "new institutionalism," Oliver E. Williamson, has emphasized the "complementarity" of transaction cost analysis with neoclassical economics. "Similarity" would have been a more accurate attribution.

While critical institutionalists are united in their rejection of the dominant economic theory, they are not so united in their treatment of the existing economic system. There are even those who would be less critical of dominant economic theory, suggesting a complementary, rather than substitute, role for institutionalism. Mention will be made of some of these in passing. Nevertheless this chapter will concentrate upon those critical institutionalists whose work has been critical of both.

HISTORICAL BACKGROUND

American institutionalism was originally called thus on account of its geographical origin and analytical focus. Its uniqueness as a tradition derives in large part from the singular contributions of Thorstein Veblen, whom many regard as its "founder." However, Veblen and his contemporaries were hardly the first to pay attention to historical change and cultural specificity. To the extent that they incorporated such factors into their works, Adam Smith and Sir James Steuart, Friedrich List and Karl Marx all qualify as institutionalists. So, too, do the members of the German historical school of economists and their American counterparts. Veblen's key theoretical innovations were to incorporate Darwinian evolutionary theory into the study of society, to develop a sophisticated theory of human behavior, and to deny the inevitability of progress. Normatively, Veblen advanced a critique of inefficiency as wrought by the institutions of contemporary capitalism. In attacking and lampooning vested interests, he laid the foundations of a theoretical tradition that systematically undermined the rationalizations employed to legitimize them.

American institutionalism did not develop in a vacuum. During the nineteenth century there had already been a number of prominent economists who had challenged the *laissez-faire* verities of the mainstream classical school, whose members believed in the existence of natural economic laws. The most prominent of these dissenters were Henry Carey (1793–1879) and Henry George (1839–97). The challenge to the dominant classical liberal ideology intensified as increasing numbers of students from the United States chose to embark on postgraduate study in Germany. The subsequent return of these had a profound influence upon the development of U.S. higher education and urban public life in general. Methods and concepts embodied in the German historical school and its Marxist offshoots were brought back to the U.S. by the new doctorates. Among those returning was Richard T. Ely (1854–1943), whose exasperation at both the turgid classical theory of the old guard of economists and the *laissez-faire* orthodoxy that ruled in practice led him to form the American Economic Association (AEA) in 1885. His original manifesto was watered down sufficiently for the AEA to embrace a plurality of perspectives, including the mainstream. Ely's attempt to engineer a qualitative change in the practice of economic inquiry became instead a professional association defined as such on the basis of scientific authority, which was itself the result of supposed value-neutrality. Ely's radical views on methodology and policy isolated him professionally, and he had difficulty gaining secure employment. Even when he did, in Madison, Wisconsin, his involvement in local labor disputes led eventually to a famous hearing in which he only narrowly avoided dismissal. He was subsequently far less critical of the *status quo*.

Nevertheless, Ely's early activism and involvement in what came to be known as the American historical school of economists (comprising mainly those returning from Germany) was important in the foundations of institutionalism. As well as authoring many books, including an influential text-book on political economy (that eventually ran to six editions) Ely also found a protégé in one of his students, John R. Commons (1862–1945).

While at Johns Hopkins University, Commons had been attracted to the study of political economy by Ely's interdisciplinary style and empirical focus. Ely's interest in labor issues, and sympathy toward the labor movement, Commons found particularly appealing. Like Ely, Commons began his academic career as a radical, and was even more unequivocal than his mentor, arguing that economists could not ignore class affiliation. This did not endear him to his contemporaries, and he, too, found it difficult to secure a tenured position. His dismissal from Syracuse University in 1899 led to Commons taking a variety of jobs, including several involving the mediation of labor disputes. Nevertheless, in 1904, Ely, having moderated his views sufficiently to have become chair of the department at Wisconsin, offered Commons a teaching post, and it was there, until 1932, that Commons built upon Ely's work to create a "school" of economists whose heterodox, empirical focus on matters of policy made them a central component of Wisconsin Governor, Robert M. La Follette's "Wisconsin idea" – that state legislation should benefit wherever possible from the input of academics employed in the state university. In this regard it is instructive that Veblen should have criticised Ely's socialism as being "paternalistic" rather than democratic.

Veblen is generally regarded as having been an unsuccessful classroom teacher. Nevertheless, he was able to nurture the intellectual development of a large number of students (as well as fellow professors). His professed favorite was Wesley Clair Mitchell (1874–1948). Together with Veblen and Commons, Mitchell is usually regarded as one of the three main founders of institutionalism. His most notable contribution was in pioneering research into business cycles, and he founded the National Bureau for Economic Research (NBER) in 1920 to advance this agenda, in so doing developing new techniques of classification, collection and analysis of macroeconomic time series data of the sort that today forms the basis of economic policy analysis and forecasting. Unlike mainstream economists, however, Mitchell tried to emulate what he regarded as Veblen's method of "analytic description," fusing together theory with discussion of related historical occurrences. He rejected orthodox economists' elevation of theory over practical relevance, placing the task of understanding actual events above the elegance of conceptual relationships. His inductivism led to charges among the mainstream that he and his acolytes preferred to present "facts without theory." This accusation became more widely applied to institutionalism as a whole. How and why did this happen?

In order to provide a satisfactory answer, it is important to recognize the singular features of what historians of economic thought usually call "American institutionalism." The attribution to Veblen, Mitchell and Commons of founder status is as much a convenience as it is a "fact." Their respective works cannot be said to cohere as part of an over-arching system or body of theory. Veblen most certainly influenced Mitchell and Commons, but Commons in particular was critical of Veblen's work. Of the three, Veblen is by far the most theoretically inclined, yet many economists designated "institutionalist" throughout the years would not have regarded themselves as belonging to a Veblenian tradition or school of thought. Veblen's radicalism was too strong for some, including the later Commons, whose faith in existing institutions such as trade unions, the state legislature and the Supreme Court contrasted significantly with Veblen's treatment of these as vested interests and/or the guardians thereof. Mitchell, meanwhile, having echoed Veblen's identification of the inadequacy of orthodox theory as an explanatory tool, devoted most of his career to empirical research that was intended to produce a comprehensive theory of business cycles. Unfortunately he died before he could complete it, and bequeathed instead fragments of this emerging theory among copious observations that served as demonstrations of a new statistical technique he had spent over two decades developing. While Mitchell and Commons attended to matters of policy, Veblen's pessimistic view of the human prospect did not lead him to formulate any programme or set of policies. The foregoing does not appear to offer a promising basis for placing these singular individuals in the same intellectual category.

Also curious is the neglect of E.R.A. Seligman, who was one of Ely's contemporaries in Germany, and was a key figure in the founding of the AEA, as well as its subsequent evolution. Seligman was instrumental in turning the AEA away from its original activist, policy-oriented approach toward an ethos of professionalism, where inquiry was conducted for its own sake, as opposed to the pursuit of a particular political agenda. This helped the cause of academic freedom in American higher education, but it also left individuals like Ely, Daniel DeLeon and Henry Carter Adams exposed when persecuted by university administrators hostile to their unhealthy interest in, and positive appraisal of, socialism. But it is as an economist that Seligman's work merits attention. In 1902 he published a series of articles that were in such demand that they were republished in book format as *The Economic Interpretation of History*. Seligman, despite his reputation as liberal reformer, was a leading scholar of Marx, and had published his methodological views as a contribution to ongoing debates surrounding the validity of the method of inquiry employed by Marx, independent of the latter's political program. Not unlike Veblen, Seligman took what he wanted from Marx while rejecting the labor theory of value. Interestingly, Seligman attempted to recover the sophistication of Marx's original treatment of inquiry from what he referred to as "vulgar Marxists" who explained everything as driven by economic interest. Instead Seligman emphasized the importance of geography as a key factor in economic development, as well as stressing the interpretive function of the base-superstructure conceptual framework, as opposed to the simple attribution of economic motives to all human action. Seligman also underlined the open-endedness of history, as opposed to the teleological determinism of those who could foresee a socialist nirvana around every corner.

In separating Marxian method from Marxian economic theory, Seligman provided much of the rationale underlying the work of Charles A. Beard, whose *Economic Interpretation of the Constitution of the United States* (1913) fundamentally altered perceptions of the Founding Fathers' motivations, and is still to be reckoned with in any appraisal of the subject. Beard is usually regarded as a political scientist who became a historian, but he is also as representative of American institutionalism as Veblen, Mitchell or Commons. One of the abiding characteristics of institutionalism as a tradition of economic thought is its openness to the insights of other social science disciplines. As these have hardened around distinct cores and become more entrenched institutionally, it has become necessary to speak of "interdisciplinarity" or "cross-disciplinary collaboration," as if "economists," "sociologists" and "political scientists" dealt with mutually exclusive areas of inquiry. If we were to apply these categories to scholars like Seligman and Beard, Veblen and Commons, we would be imposing present-day notions of these upon circumstances in which their meaning would have been very different. American institutionalism was an eclectic approach to economic inquiry that took little heed of the artificial constraints imposed by academic convention.

The first attempt to define institutionalism as a distinct approach to economic inquiry was made by Walton H. Hamilton (1881–1958) in his December 1918 address to the AEA. Like Ely over thirty years before, Hamilton attempted to provide a manifesto for change. He identified five central characteristics of institutionalism:

1. Institutionalists have greater concern for relevance than for logical consistency *per se*. As a result, their work is often explicitly oriented towards policy.

2. Institutionalists employ the insights of other academic social science disciplines, including sociology, anthropology and psychology, in order to provide a richer analysis of both institutions and human behavior.

3. An understanding of institutions and their centrality to the social and political economy is essential. This understanding should encompass their formation, preservation, evolution and decline.

4. The economy is not a separate system obeying universal laws, but is a socially embedded entity, enmeshed in the history, politics and culture of societies, the natural environment, and technological change.

5. Similarly, individuals act in a social context, influenced by and influencing the history, politics and culture of their respective societies. Therefore the orthodox assumption of agents as rational utility-maximizers is rejected.

Hamilton's principles still hold good today. As they demonstrate, institutionalists' primary dispute with neoclassical economists is methodological. This accounts for the broad spectrum of institutionalist opinion with regard to policy. Of course there are mainstream economists, too, who employ neoclassical techniques to advance policies that are of the Left. But it is no accident that most "economic reasoning" is in fact justification for privatization, marketization, commodification – the reduction of human existence to market relationships. The large financial awards given to research foundations, think tanks, and individual economists all to support the advocacy of "free market" solutions, thereby lending them "scientific" legitimacy, are no mere coincidence.

Of course, a major attraction of neoclassical economics is its high level of abstraction, which enables those who enjoy solving puzzles to construct elaborate (or not so elaborate) hypothetical problem situations and thereafter generate solutions whose outcome was a foregone conclusion given the premises of the respective problems. Compared to advancing particular policy agendas this intellectual pursuit is relatively harmless, but desperately unproductive. Other than the publication of scholarly papers of little consequence beyond the career advancement of the academic concerned, few can be said to benefit from this rather costly exercise. As John Kenneth Galbraith once said, "Economics is extremely useful as a form of employment for economists."

Nevertheless, neoclassical economists often serve overtly ideological ends. Possibly the most notorious of these in recent times was the role of economists in administering "shock therapy" to the former Soviet Union. Those responsible for what is now universally acknowledged as a catastrophe naively assumed that the "core institutions" of capitalism required to be established, and thereafter everything else would follow (as suggested by North). Revealingly, and contrary to the oft-incanted rhetoric of "free markets and democracy," the former took precedence over the latter, as concurrent privatizations and withdrawals of state supports impacted negatively on ordinary living standards, thus breeding political opposition. This was first overruled by the drafting of a new Russian constitution under which presidential decree (or, more accurately, diktat) took precedence over the customary forms of liberal democracy such as parliamentary debate and scrutiny. Thus, the reformers could usurp the authority of the presidency to railroad through their reforms free of accountability to the wider constituency most affected by these. When even this proved to be insufficient as guarantee of untrammeled power, tanks were deployed to sack the Duma in 1993. The current president, Vladimir Putin, is presently attracting criticism for his apparent authoritarianism. Markedly little is being said by way of acknowledging the institutional configuration that enables him to be authoritarian, nor of those responsible for bequeathing it.

Whether for reasons of ideology or simply naive scientism, the debacle of shock therapy has amply demonstrated the limitations of abstracted theory. While the economists responsible did have a clear goal (however crude) informing their actions, they had little conception of the means by which to achieve that goal. Not only did they lack an adequate theory of institutional adjustment, but, more fundamentally, they had no adequate conception of institution. The latter deficiency lies at the heart of differences between neoclassical economists and institutionalists.

EARLY INSTITUTIONALIST THEORY

So what is an institution? Not surprisingly, there have been many efforts made to define the concept. Writing in 1909, Veblen defined institutions as "settled habits of thought common to the generality of men." A more recent definition states: "An economic *institution* is a cluster of mores that configures power or authority over things and people that are relevant to the material and social continuity of human life" (Stanfield, 1996 p.132). While more elaborate attempts have been made, these capture the essence of the problems inherent in the neoclassical approach to (or ignorance of) institutions. Far from being simply a set of rules imposed externally upon individuals (who, as rational utility-maximizers, are presumed to respond to such rules in wholly predictable fashion), institutions are complex entities that are internalized and shared. They are the products of historical development, and culturally embedded, being responses to problems that require collective action. Examples include the legal system, marriage and religious custom.

Conservatives of a certain philosophical strain place great value upon tradition precisely because they regard it as aggregated human wisdom collected over generations in response to perennial problems. It is a measure of how far language can be stretched that many avowed "conservatives" today preach the very policies that would undermine the traditions to which they pledge adherence. As Marx well understood, capitalist development uproots tradition and imposes a different order upon societies, often with great violence. This was certainly true of the former Soviet Union. It is also true of the capitalist countries themselves, where *laissez-faire* socioeconomic policies and relentless privatization combine to lower and eventually remove the social safety net necessary for the continuities vital to the recreation of community and family, the very institutions so honored by "conservatives."

Veblen often took a very dim view of institutions, on one occasion describing them as "imbecilic." This was not because Veblen viewed all continuity as undesirable. Rather, it was his commentary on the transformation of practical technologies intended to solve real problems into impractical, inefficient institutions that render human behavior ceremonial. This recurring phenomenon was, and is, due to the formation and embedding of what he termed "vested interests" whose purpose was to enshrine privilege and invidious distinction at the expense of the "underlying population" (Veblen's analogue of Marx's working class).

Veblen's dichotomy of technology and institutions was adapted by Clarence E. Ayres (1891–1972) in his most accomplished work, *The Theory of Economic Progress* (1944). Ayres emphasized the instrumental functions of technology as against the ceremonialism of institutions. In this he was primarily concerned to refute religious and ideological belief, as he was a true adherent of the Enlightenment faith in human reason. While Veblen's criticisms of institutions were based upon an evaluative criterion of efficiency, Ayres equated "institutions" with ceremonialism; they were the embodiment of entrenched privilege and invidious distinction, and therefore obstructed technological progress, itself the key to economic progress. This sharp dualism contrasts with Veblen's more sophisticated recognition of the simultaneous instrumentality and ceremonialism inherent in social institutions. Ayres' schema implied the assignment of mutually exclusive categories to institutions, when in fact, as the latter evolve, the proportion of each attribute present in their manifest functioning changes. As a pessimist Veblen anticipated the gradual usurping of the instrumental function by the ceremonial as being almost inevitable, but he did not treat these functions as dualistic – that is to say, mutually exclusive. Rather, Veblen saw instrumentality and ceremonialism as organically related and even mutually supportive, as well as conflicting.

According to Ayres, economic development is the result of the innate human propensity to solve problems. His notion of technology as problem-solving tools was, however, Eurocentric. Veblen had highlighted the continuities between the modern capitalist state and the predatory, dynastic state of feudalism. Ayres applied his simplified treatment of institutions to his reading of history, in which European technology spread all over the world. "Development" was most pronounced where cultural resistance was least. Some readers may find that euphemistic in the extreme, especially as applied to North America and Australia. As for Africa, according to this reading indigenous culture must have been too strong for European ingenuity to take root. Ayres effectively excuses the violence perpetrated upon other peoples in the name of "civilization." This is not to say that Ayres was intentionally or consciously racist, itself a concept subject to flux, but it does highlight the limitations of a particular form of American exceptionalism which, however enlightened it may consider itself to be, is far too casual in its treatment of history. We may argue, on Ayres' own terms, that his was an implicitly invidious distinction made with regard to the victims of Western imperialism.

Ayres was no champion of capitalism, and thought that its institutions would wither in the face of the irrefutable truth of science. Despite his disavowal of historical certainty, his optimism was powerful enough to overcome whatever doubts he may have had about the ability of human reason to solve problems. For Ayres scientific discovery – the application of the values of science to all branches of inquiry – would render the ceremonial attachment to free market ideology anachronistic. As it drove on economic development, so scientific progress would drive out the predatory and invidious features of capitalism and bequeathe a society not dissimilar to the soviet of engineers postulated by Veblen in *The Engineers and the Price System* (1921): except that Veblen was engaging in satire, while Ayres firmly believed in the liberal values of the Enlightenment. That he could do so despite McCarthyism (of which he, himself, was a victim), the Jim Crow South (in which he lived and worked for most of his career) and the proliferation of nuclear weapons amid an international politics of paranoia, culminating in the Cuban missile crisis of 1962, is perplexing, to say the least.

Ayres was an inspiring teacher to many, whether in the classroom or on paper. Of those working in the middle years of the twentieth century, few did more to perpetuate Veblen's legacy, despite their clear theoretical differences. Ayres misread Veblen with respect to conceptualizing institutions. Nevertheless, it was also Ayres who correctly identified the similarities between Veblen and the philosopher John Dewey (1859–1952). Both argued for an explicitly scientific treatment of social problems; both viewed history as an evolutionary process with no determinate end; both viewed human nature not as given but as emergent within a specific historical and cultural milieu; both treated means and ends as mutually informative and continuously evolving. In recognizing these shared characteristics in the work of Veblen and Dewey, Ayres established a basis for further theoretical development that became a central feature of Veblenian critical institutionalist inquiry.

Nevertheless, the almost cavalier fashion in which Ayres dispensed with institutions led his successors to modify the prescription somewhat. This is evident in the work of John Fagg Foster (1907–85), who was acutely aware of the social upheaval occasioned by economic development. According to Foster, human nature is such that its inherent inventiveness and creativity ensure the inevitability of change, and thereby the emergence of new social problems. In this he could agree with Ayres, whose depiction of human life as a "tool process" was based on a belief in human ingenuity, itself the result of the physical and mental endowments marking out humanity from the rest of the natural world. Unlike Ayres, however, Foster foresaw problems with a relentless drive to innovate, not least the painful and counterproductive disruption this often entailed. With change a given, the fundamental problem for Foster was one of how to ensure that institutional adjustments are consistent with the rest of the institutional configuration. Since institutions serve both instrumental and ceremonial ends, the task was to identify the means necessary to serving the end of increasing institutions' instrumentality without unintentionally hindering that of others elsewhere.

Foster examined closely the problem of institutional adjustment, distilling three vital aspects. Firstly, adjustment is required where the existing institutional configurations do not fulfill the generic ends of life alluded to by Veblen. How that adjustment is to be achieved is dependent upon technology which, in an adaptation of Dewey's formulation, is itself determined by the state of what Dewey termed "warranted knowledge" – outcomes of inquiry directed toward the achievement of the ends sought with the means identified, based on the strongest available evidence. This renders all such outcomes provisional or tentative – just as today's strongest evidence may be supplanted by even more robust findings tomorrow, so too does the institutional configuration requiring adjustment evolve. While there may be ultimate ends to be regarded as axiomatic, their accomplishment is attained via that of intermediate goals, which are themselves part of a relationship of mutual dependence with the means of their achievement. In other words, unlike the mainstream of Western thought, institutionalism follows a fellow American intellectual tradition, philosophical pragmatism, in asserting the symbiosis of means and ends. If anything, such a position recognizes the oxymoronic nature of regimes that would impose democracy by diktat, or of movements that would proclaim the sanctity of human life whilst allowing it to wither. This is consonant with Foster's second principle of institutional adjustment: the recognition of the interdependence of the components comprising the institutional configuration. For changes to achieve their desired effect, the implications they would have upon the rest of the institutional fabric must be anticipated.

Any process of change involves threats to vested interests

which can be expected to engage in rearguard actions, if not pre-emptive strikes. Difficulties of whatever complexion that arise unexpectedly can deprive change of the necessary momentum and support, even without the opposition of vested interests. This leads to Foster's third principle, that of minimal dislocation. According to Foster, the magnitude and rate of institutional change must be capable of being incorporated by that part of the configuration otherwise unaltered. If it is not, the desired changes will only lead to further disruption and discontent. This has been demonstrated most graphically in the former Soviet Union, as mentioned above, but for those concerned to move beyond capitalism as a definitive means of social organization, how can the principle of minimal dislocation be reconciled with the institutionalized injustices and cruelties that are endemic to capitalism?

Those adhering to a revolutionary political program will find Foster's prescriptions utterly inadequate: a reformist sop to capitalism. However, the kind of historical materialism that borders on, if not equates to, economic determinism ignores the important cultural aspects of social life that cannot simply be eradicated once and for all by the overthrow of a particular regime. Just as the Russian Orthodox Church, anti-Semitism and nationalism all survived the Soviet experience very much intact, so too would reference to capitalist cultural modes in Western societies linger beyond any once-and-for-all fundamental change. Foster's principles of institutional adjustment highlight such probabilities and so provide a robust analytical framework. However, they are more problematic when considering incremental reforms – the very changes that they are intended to assist. This is because Foster offers no specific directions beyond the abstract principles outlined above. In all fairness it would be unreasonable to expect otherwise, given the multifarious types and evolutionary nature of social institutions and their configurations. At best, Foster's principles are guidelines that can assist those wishing to effect economic and political change.

Once again, however, the absence of any awareness of the role of imperialism and slavery in U.S. capitalist development mars Foster's legacy. Foster did not leave much by way of a written corpus – his was primarily an oral tradition. Neverthe-less what fragments there were of theoretical development in his papers were collected and published in a special volume of the *Journal of Economic Issues* in 1981 (more recently, Marc R. Tool has presented Foster's thought as a unified whole – see Tool 2000). In one paper in which he surveyed the various schools of economic thought, he attributed to institutionalism a specificity founded upon "the peculiarities of the American experience," not least that of the "frontier":

> The frontier experience and the attitudes and realizations arising from it disinclined Americans not only toward invidious distinc-tions, but also toward the acceptance of any particular institutional structure as perpetual .... They generally came to regard institu-tional structures as devices or means of carrying on the various functions of the social process, including the economic function. In their thinking, the functions became the continuing factors, and all institutional structures became subject to adjustment.

If one were white and of European descent, then the rejection of old country mores perpetuating hierarchy and invidious distinc-tion, as these applied to white Europeans, was arguably a strong feature in the cultural formation of what became the United States of America. However, the treatment meted out to indigenous Americans and imported African slaves would suggest, at the very least, a rather more tenacious form of invidious distinction than Foster admitted. While there is a strong current of populism in U.S. political culture (derived from the Jeffersonian tradition), its ambiguity with regard to what is to be done after the removal of whatever robber barons or heartless business leaders can be divined from the common ground shared by avowedly different campaigners like Ralph Nader and Patrick J. Buchanan. Nor does Foster leave unequivo-cal direction concerning which takes priority: the removal of invidious distinction or the principle of minimal dislocation. For this tension to be resolved one would have to assume the existence of a society in which the problems of racism, extreme inequality, poverty and gender discrimination were much less pronounced than they are in reality.

The neglect of racism was a common aspect in the work of those otherwise critical of American capitalism. C. Wright Mills (1916–62), a former student of Ayres, had, during the 1950s, published a series of books that marked him out from the rest of the discipline of sociology as one dissatisfied with both mainstream theory and practice, as well as deeply critical of U.S. politics and society. *The Power Elite* (1956) examined the interlocking relationships connecting the state, business and the military, as well as the methods employed to perpetuate these. *The Sociological Imagination* (1959) meanwhile was a rallying cry to all students of social science to break free of what he called the "methodological inhibition" and instead engage in relevant, challenging research. As has been argued by Rick Tilman, Mills is representative of the American institutionalist tradition, but even Mills could be, and was, criticized for his neglect of racism. Herbert Aptheker, an otherwise sympathetic Marxist critic of Mills, identified the latter's "blind spot concerning the whole matter of the Negro" as an "especially glaring" omission.

It is clear from the above that there are elements of the intellectual legacy of institutionalism that are deeply troubling. The complacency regarding other cultures fallen victim to the predatory imperialism of Western "civilization," and a related belief in the intrinsic superiority of the "American way," however flawed, together with general ignorance of the problem of racism, itself deeply institutionalized, detracts from the telling criticisms leveled by institutionalists at both mainstream economic thought and economic policies.

That said, dissatisfaction with both mainstream economics and doctrinaire forms of Marxism led a number of European economists to engage in a fruitful dialogue with American institutionalism. In the process, they have helped it become less "American" whilst refining its critical edge.

EUROPEAN INSTITUTIONALISTS

We have already noted the European antecedents of American institutionalism. Not surprisingly, as it has become a recognized tradition of economic inquiry, there have been Europeans who have consciously appropriated parts of it in their own work, while others have been shown in retrospect to possess clear intellectual affinities with institutionalism.

Perhaps the earliest European economist to take more than a passing interest in institutionalism was John A. Hobson (1858–1940). Hobson not only corresponded with Veblen, but even wrote an admiring book on his work, *Veblen* (1936). Meanwhile Veblen found much to admire in Hobson's *Imperialism: A Study* (1902). Yet Hobson was too idiosyncratic to be easily pigeonholed as an institutionalist, incorporating as he did elements of orthodox economic theory into his own formulations.

Probably the first and most prominent of the European contributors to institutionalism was the Swede, Gunnar Myrdal (1898–1987). Originally hostile toward institutionalism, Myrdal nevertheless was also skeptical of the claims of value-neutrality made by mainstream economists like Ludwig von Mises and Lionel Robbins. Though published in 1953, Myrdal's *The Political Element in the Development of Economic Theory* was based on lectures delivered in 1931 and made short shrift of the scientific status accorded to mainstream economics by mainstream economists. Rejecting the possibility of value-neutrality, and highlighting the metaphysical and teleological assumptions underpinning neoclassical economics, Myrdal argued that values were central to any purposeful inquiry, framing both the perceived problem situation and the methods undertaken to resolve it. Neoclassical economists, by affecting a "scientific" pose, were appealing to secular authority in much the same way as theocrats might appeal to divine authority in justifying otherwise untenable claims.

Myrdal's most famous work is *An American Dilemma: The Negro Problem and Modern Democracy* (1944). Within and even beyond the institutionalist canon, it remains the outstanding contribution to the study of race and racism in U.S. capitalist development. Myrdal examined the various factors – economic, political, social, cultural and historical – to do with institutionalized racism, and mapped their configuration as it impacted upon African Americans. Thus could Myrdal explain the complexity of this enduring problem. Myrdal himself later

attributed to this work his own identification with institutionalism.

Unfortunately Myrdal did not herald a legion of institutionalists specializing in the analysis of racism. This is remarkable,
given the centrality of an egalitarian ethos that disavows
hierarchy and invidious distinction. Among those working to
rectify this lacuna today is Steven Shulman who reiterates the
strengths that an institutionalist approach to the study of
racism would possess:

> In addition to its attention to cultural norms, positive feedback
> effects, and evolutionary holism, institutionalism is uniquely suited
> to racial analysis due to its emphasis on the problem of power ...
> [T]he exercise of power which subordinates blacks is complex due to
> the interaction of class relations and race relations. Racism may
> benefit both capitalists and white workers in particular ways, and it
> may hurt both of them in particular ways. The distributional
> consequences of discrimination may vary between historical periods
> and economic contexts. Furthermore, power is embedded in the
> hierarchical structure of organizations, and as such is a component
> in the social relations of both class and race. The instrumental
> values which institutionalists advocate provide a normative basis for
> a critique of the exercise of power, including white supremacy.
> (Shulman in Dugger, 1996 p. 268)

Myrdal, meanwhile, also further developed the theory of cumulative causation already present in the work of Veblen and Ayres
by applying it to the study of economic development. With its
emphasis upon equilibrium, mainstream economics cannot
grapple with the problems of poorer countries which, despite all
the apparent help, remain mired in poverty and underdevelopment. The imposition of structural adjustment policies by the
neoclassical economists of the World Bank and International
Monetary Fund throughout the 1980s and 1990s has been a
brutal lesson in the inadequacy of both the obsession with
equilibrium, and the idea that U.S. norms can be simply
replicated on a global scale. Myrdal demonstrated that institutional changes have a momentum that takes with it the rest of
the configuration. Thus development in one area can produce

"backwash effects" in others, as resources are sucked toward the growth center. In our era of ever-greater global integration, such cumulative processes can produce ever-wider disparities in economic welfare between the developed and less developed countries. Indeed, they have done just that.

Especially since the publication of Rachel Carson's *Silent Spring* in 1962, human activities' destructive consequences upon the natural environment have attracted ever-greater attention. Yet it was over a decade earlier that a German economist, K. William Kapp (1910–76) published his seminal work, *The Social Costs of Private Enterprise* (1950). Kapp focused upon what mainstream economists refer to as "externalities" – the public consequences of private exchange. Most orthodox economists typically assume that capitalist forms of organization generate positive externalities: that is, as well as achieving better, more efficient allocations of scarce resources, capitalism is, if not its ultimate expression, the nearest approximation to human freedom. Kapp demonstrated that this was far from the case. For all its vaunted efficiency, capitalism enabled powerful corporations and individuals to avoid picking up the tab for the costly consequences of their business activities. Thus the pollution of air, water and land, the unsightly degradation of natural beauty by architectural monstrosities, the routine dangers faced and injuries borne by workers (including occupational diseases and fatalities), as well as the psychological costs of laboring under capitalism (fear of unemployment, wage slavery, alienation) were all systematically excluded by both economists and accountants. This was made possible by the emphasis placed upon individual freedom and private exchange. Socializing the costs of private enterprise was, and is, an effective means of improving "economic performance" as it is defined under capitalist criteria. As Kapp himself wrote,

To dismiss these phenomena as "noneconomic" because they occur outside the market complex is possible but neither ingenuous nor tenable in view of the fact that, apart from their obviously human aspect, they have a price for both the individual and society. [Meanwhile] a system of decision-making operating in accordance with the principle of investment for profit cannot be expected to proceed in any way other than by trying to reduce its costs whenever possible and by ignoring those losses that can be shifted to third persons or to society at large.

RESPONSES TO CORPORATE POWER

Veblen's analysis of the modern corporation as an inherently contradictory enterprise formed the basis of subsequent institutionalist analysis of business organization. Some of this has been optimistic; the rest has not, sometimes most emphatically.

The work of Robert A. Brady (1901–63) is a powerful example of the latter tendency. Influenced mainly by Veblen and John Maurice Clark (1884–1963), another notable institutionalist, Brady spent time in Germany during the 1920s studying its economic rationalization movement, the process whereby the restructuring of German industry produced cartels, state coordination and integrated planning. This prepared him well for his subsequent analysis of Nazi Germany, *The Spirit and Structure of German Fascism* (1937), the first, and still among the very best, studies of Nazism (leading to his designation as "prematurely" anti-fascist). Thereafter he was led to examine the economic development of France, Britain, the United States, Italy and Japan in parallel to that of Germany, resulting in *Business as a System of Power* (1943).

Brady found that fascism was not some aberration, but a logical outgrowth of capitalist development under particular circumstances. Not surprisingly, Germany, Italy and Japan were identified as having evolved into fascist states. Less predictably, Brady showed that by 1939 France, too, was moving closely toward its own version of fascism. The relative lack of capital–labor discord in Britain and the United States, resulting in part from its mitigation by the organs of the state, prevented, according to Brady, a similar outcome. The common trajectory of capitalist states during the 1920s and 1930s resulted from depressed economic conditions and the responses of business leaders to these. In every case greater emphasis was placed upon consolidation and concentration of business power, in such a way that the state itself was subject to ever greater manipulation. In the fascist countries this backfired, in that the regimes helped into power by business leaders turned on the latter as state goals took priority. But where a more "friendly fascism" (to use the title of Bertram Gross's 1980 book analyzing the United States) prevailed, the influence of big business remained pernicious. The ideological camouflage of anti-statism, reactivated during the Reagan/ Thatcher era, only obscures the reality of state-monopoly capital symbiosis typical of contemporary capitalism.

John Kenneth Galbraith (1908–) represents a more optimistic tendency within institutionalism. Although severely critical of mainstream economic theory and policy, and an acute observer of the contradictions of capitalism, he is nonetheless rather less of a radical in his policy prescriptions. This is because these are based upon what he regards as a "realistic" assessment of what is achievable. His long association with the Democratic Party and service to four Democratic Presidents (Roosevelt, Truman, Kennedy and Johnson) served to temper his critical edge and instead nurture a yen for pragmatic solutions. This is evidenced most recently in his pessimistic appraisal of the contemporary United States published as *The Culture of Contentment* (1992). His subsequent *The Good Society* (1996) offered a set of proposals that were substantially diluted versions of policies that he had advocated in the 1970s (though still more radical than mainstream political discourse would allow).

In *The New Industrial State* (1967), Galbraith suggested that the Marxist progression of power from land, to capital, and finally, to labor, was wrong. Power would reside ultimately in organization. The demands placed upon corporations intent upon minimizing uncertainty were such that the ability to manage information was more essential than ever before. To this end a cadre of skilled workers that Galbraith termed the "technostructure" had been developed in order to accumulate, process and interpret the myriad data that modern corporations and states required in order to function successfully. The problem for capitalists, however, was that their pecuniary prerogative would be undermined by the ethos of efficiency possessed by members of the technostructure, educated as they were in universities where liberal values reigned. Reliance upon those whose value systems were very different from those of pecuniary culture would lead to the transformation of society into a more benign, egalitarian form of capitalism. Subsequent events led Galbraith to bemoan his lack of foresight in this matter, as the era of Margaret Thatcher and Ronald Reagan heralded an unprecedented embedding of the pecuniary culture at the expense of whatever alternatives may have been expected to challenge it. Accordingly, the later Galbraith has assumed the more detached, pessimistic mantle of his mentor, Veblen, whilst retaining a commitment to policy prescription, albeit far less ambitious than before.

Continuing in the tradition of Veblen, Ayres and Foster, whilst incorporating the insights of Kapp, Myrdal, Galbraith and others, Marc R. Tool (1921–) has furthered the development of institutionalist theory. Published relatively late in his career, *The Discretionary Economy* (1979, recently reissued) stands as a rigorous effort to bring up to date the institutionalist theory of contemporary capitalism and offer a framework for the reconstruction of society toward a democratic, participatory ideal.

Tool's has been the most systematic effort to incorporate Dewey's theory of inquiry into the methodology of institutionalism. Far more comprehensively than Ayres, Tool has emphasized the democratic component of Dewey's philosophy as fundamental to scientific endeavor. This is especially important as regards social inquiry, where political and ideological beliefs are inextricably bound up with the subjects, objects and process of inquiry. To deny this is to mislead. Mainstream economists' equation of objectivity with neutrality is a fallacy, an example of what William Dugger later termed an "enabling myth." Galbraith is remembered for coining the phrase "conventional wisdom," descriptive of mainstream economic thought. The effect is to belittle unimaginative economists content to accept, unquestioningly, the main tenets of their discipline. The idea of enabling myth exposes to greater scrutiny the purposeful use of commonly accepted notions as cover for processes and actions whose consequences might otherwise lead to rejection of the *status quo*, thereby threatening vested interests. The enabling myth of value-neutrality allows economists to eschew all appearance of interest in the practical outcomes of their theories and policies. Natural laws are invoked in a secular version of recourse to divine authority so beloved of demagogues, clerical and lay. In this way people are assured that "there is no alternative," and that we must, regardless of how unpleasant or undesirable, proceed as ordained.

In this way Tool refocuses Ayres' rejection of the ceremonial away from the pre-modern and toward the ways in which present-day vested interests legitimize their privilege. Where Ayres rejects primitivism, Tool rejects elitism.

Tool does agree with Ayres that in the development and use of technology is to be found value (in contrast to the "explanations" of orthodox price theory) but, while Ayres, following his "misreading" of Veblen, treats idle machines and misapplied knowledge as inefficient in their own right, Tool again refocuses on the social impact of such problems. The social and economic consequences of unemployment, underemployment, poverty and alienation include the denial of the full development of human personality and community, something Tool describes as "inefficiency of monumental proportions." To this end Tool has employed the notion of "real income," going far beyond that subject to pecuniary measurement. Echoing W.E.B. DuBois' conceptualization of institutionalized racism as resulting in unequal rewards for whites and blacks in both economic and non-economic terms, Tool has taken account of the supposedly "non-economic" effects of invidious distinction in order to highlight their economic impact. Chief among these is the access, or lack of it, to the levers of power.

CONCLUSION

Writing in 1981, Marc Tool identified a "compulsive shift to institutional analysis" where the limitations of neoclassical dogma would become ever more apparent, leading economists of all stripes to seek alternatives that were more historically relevant and yielding greater theoretical insights and more truly efficient policy outcomes. Non-critical institutionalists, desperate to retain the "credibility" of neoclassical economics, have advanced very little down this road. Meanwhile more students, teachers, and the just plain interested, are recognizing that true understanding of economic reality requires far more than a mastery of techniques designed to yield optimal results in make-believe worlds. In the academic sphere, the denial of space to non-neoclassical forms of economics means that critical institutionalist political economy is now often to be found in the domain of political science.

Critical institutionalism, as a category of thought, contains within itself many shades of criticism. This chapter has focused on certain elements within this tradition that are more critical in their analyses of contemporary capitalism than are certain others. Limitations of space have prevented discussion of commonalities between critical institutionalists and those working within Marxian and other traditions. The monopoly capital school (see Chapter 5) shares certain similarities with the work of Veblen and Galbraith, for example, while James O'Connor, Ian Gough and Claus Offe have produced theory and analysis that bears strong affinities with those of Veblen and Kapp. Of late, institutionalists such as William Dugger and James Ronald Stanfield have attempted to engage in constructive dialogue with Marxian writers as part of an effort to delineate a specifically radical institutionalism. Brady and Mills were early examples of such radicals, and have been followed, most consciously with regard to Brady, by Douglas Dowd and R. Jeffrey Lustig. The proto-feminism of Veblen and Galbraith is being succeeded by new work that highlights the unique problems faced by women under capitalism. Janice Peterson and Paulette Olson are among those advancing this line of institutionalist inquiry. Other writers, not consciously working in a Veblenian "American institutionalist" tradition, but no less critical or institutionalist, include William Lazonick and David Coates.

Critical institutionalism is a multi-faceted collection of theoretical approaches to the study of capitalism. Its constituent parts are united by a commitment both to theorizing that is historically relevant and to the treatment of history as an evolutionary process with no pre-ordained end. Capitalism is viewed neither as the inevitable product of human progress nor the pinnacle of human achievement. It is an historically contingent configuration of social institutions, a product of human action, that can be altered according to human design. The egalitarian ethos of critical institutionalism makes its practitioners naturally critical of a system that produces so much by way of invidious distinction. The major fault line between critical institutionalists lies between those who believe that the current system can be made to work better (that is, to effect a greater redistribution of real income) or whether capitalism itself is capable of such a transformation. The best work in this tradition retains Veblen's two strongest qualities – his scientific objectivity and his rejection of endemic invidious distinction – without succumbing to the despair that rendered all hope of a brighter tomorrow forlorn.

REFERENCES

Barrow, Clyde W. (2000) *More Than a Historian: The Political and Economic Thought of Charles A. Beard*. New Brunswick, NJ and London: Transaction Publishers.

Brady, Robert A. (2001) *Business as a System of Power*. New Brunswick, NJ and London: Transaction Publishers.

Coates, David (2000) *Models of Capitalism: Growth and Stagnation in the Modern Era*. Cambridge: Polity Press.

Dugger, William M., ed. (1996) *Inequality: Radical Institutionalist Views on Race, Gender, Class and Nation*. Westport, CT: Greenwood Press.

Galbraith, John Kenneth (1998) *The Affluent Society*, 40th anniversary edition. Boston: Houghton Mifflin.

Gruchy, Allan G. (1987) *The Reconstruction of Economics: An Analysis of the Fundamentals of Institutional Economics*. Westport, CT: Greenwood Press.

Hodgson, Geoffrey M. (1999) *Economics and Utopia: Why the Learning Economy is not the End of History*. London and New York: Routledge.

Lazonick, William (1991) *Business Organization and the Myth of the Market Economy*. Cambridge: Cambridge University Press.

Stanfield, James Ronald (1996) *John Kenneth Galbraith*. London: Macmillan; New York: St. Martin's Press.

Tilman, Rick (1984) *C. Wright Mills: A Native Radical and his American Intellectual Roots*. University Park, PA and London: Pennsylvania State University Press.

Tool, Marc R. (2000) *Value Theory and Economic Progress: The Institutional Economics of J. Fagg Foster*. Boston: Kluwer Academic Publishers.

Tool, Marc R. (2001) *The Discretionary Economy: A Normative Theory of Political Economy*. New Brunswick, NJ and London: Transaction Publishers.

The main source of current critical institutionalist thought is the *Journal of Economic Issues*.

5 POST KEYNESIAN ECONOMICS (1930–2000): An Emerging Heterodox Economic Theory of Capitalism

Frederic S. Lee

INTRODUCTION

There are numerous economic theories that attempt to explain how contemporary capitalism works. The one accepted by most economists is neoclassical economics, and its identifying features are that markets always work, all prices and quantities are determined by supply and demand, the more individuals save the better off the economy is, and consumer choice drives all economic activity. In contrast to this "capitalism is the best of all possible worlds" are Marxian and Institutional economics which characterize current capitalism as "not the best of all possible worlds."

Marxists and Institutionalists reject the identifying features of neoclassical economics along with their underlying theory. However, their explanations of capitalism are also flawed in some respects. For example, both the Marxian theory of value (or prices) and profits and the Institutionalist explanation for the level of economic activity in the economy as a whole are problematical. Post Keynesian economics is a third alternative to neoclassical economics that avoids the drawbacks of Marxism and Institutionalism. Like them, it explains how contemporary capitalism works, using a body of theory that is consciously, point for point, and concept for concept, antithetical to neoclassical economics. Moreover, because Post Keynesian economics incorporates many of the important components of Marxism and Institutionalism, its explanations of capitalism, while theoretically more sound, are not vastly different from theirs. Thus, Post Keynesians see their work as a theoretical and explanatory advance over the other "schools."

Post Keynesian economics is a body of theory that is used by economists to construct historical narratives – that is, stories of how contemporary capitalism works. The historical narratives do not simply recount or superficially describe actual economic events, such as the exploitation of workers; they do more in that they *explain analytically* the internal workings of the historical economic process that, say, generates the exploitation of workers. What the stories tell do not pre-determine the future – which is for people to make, although (given the existing structures and causal mechanisms), as Marx has put it, "not to their own choosing." Because the Post Keynesian narratives provide an accurate picture of how contemporary capitalism actually works, the choice of future paths is, at least, clearer. More specifically, the Post Keynesians can use their theory and narratives to suggest what paths future economic events might take and propose relevant economic policies. In constructing these narratives, Post Keynesians have, at the same time, constructed a social–economic–political picture of capitalism; and the focus of this picture is the vision that Post Keynesians have of capitalism.

Post Keynesian economics, as a community of economists supporting the same common body of theory, emerged in the 1970s. However, although many of its theoretical ideas can be traced back to Adam Smith, David Ricardo, and Karl Marx, the Great Depression of the 1930s is its true starting point. This economic, social, and political disaster prompted some economists to begin to question conventional modes of economic thinking.

In 1935 Gardiner Means, an American economist working in Franklin Roosevelt"s New Deal, noted that in industries where enterprises were large and therefore had market power, prices were administered to the market independently of supply and demand; and, conversely, in industries where enterprises were small, prices were determined in the market through the interaction of supply and demand. Hence, administered prices were relatively inflexible in face of a decline in demand while market prices readily declined in face of a decline in demand. As a consequence, the administered price industries experienced significant declines in production and sales in contrast to the market price industries where production and sales had relatively small declines.

Means backed up his argument with extensive data on prices, production enterprise size, and the degree of concentration in American industries; taken together the data highlighted administered prices and their disruptive impact on the American economy. The theoretical importance of Means's argument was that prices did not coordinate economic activity or allocate resources, as claimed by neoclassical economists. Thus, Means argued, a new picture or theory of economic relationships was needed.

At this same time, economists at Oxford University began an empirical investigation of two economic questions: do interest rates affect business decisions to invest? Do enterprises adjust their prices in light of the business cycle? The investigation consisted of an invitation by Oxford economists to businessmen to visit Oxford for interviews. From the interviews it was discovered that the interest rate had little or no impact on investment decisions, a highly significant result but one that had little effect on economists at that time. They also discovered that businessmen did not set prices by supply and demand, as depicted by neoclassical economics. Instead they used full cost pricing procedures where prices were set by adding a profit mark-up to costs. The significance of the finding was that prices were clearly set independently of market forces and not with the view of maximizing profits. The combination of Means's administered price argument with Oxford's full cost pricing suggested that businessmen, prices, markets, and the economy behaved in ways critically different from those depicted in neoclassical economic theory.

In 1936 *The General Theory of Employment, Interest, and Money* by John Maynard Keynes, a Cambridge economist, was published. It quickly had an impact on the thinking of economists and, within a few years, on the formulation of economic policy. While the policy impact is important, the significance of *The General Theory* for Post Keynesian economics lies in its revolutionary theoretical arguments. Because of the Great Depression, Keynes was concerned with understanding and delineating the factors that determined the level of output and employment. Neoclassical economists argued that savings determined investment, which in turn determined output and employment. Keynes, on the other hand, argued that effective demand – that is, private investment and government expenditure – determined output and employment while savings adjusted to investment. Moreover, he diminished the role of the interest rate in coordinating investment and savings and had its determination located in the financial markets. In addition, with the interest rate being determined in the financial markets, Keynes conceived the economy as a monetary rather than a barter economy. Finally he argued that uncertainty, conceived in term of the future being unknowable, was an inherent feature of a monetary economy and hence affected all business decisions. These four innovations produced a number of theoretical surprises. The first was that money mattered in a monetary economy, in that financial activities had a real impact on economic activity. Secondly, effective demand rather than prices or the interest rate coordinated economic activity, allocated resources in the economy, and determined output and employment. Thirdly, the entrepreneur's desire to invest, rather than the interest rate, had the dominant impact upon business investment decisions. Lastly there was no market mechanism that would ensure that effective demand would be sufficient to drive a capitalist economy towards the full utilization of its resources and the employment of labor. Instead full employment could only be achieved through the intervention of an outside social, that is a non-market, institution, such as the state.

At the same time Keynes was writing his *General Theory*, a Polish economist, Michal Kalecki, was reaching the same conclusions using, however, a Marxian class analysis that distinguished between workers and capitalists, and a degree of monopoly pricing model. The importance of his work was that Kalecki linked the class system to the performance of the economy and the degree of monopoly (or later known as the 'profit mark-up') at the micro-level to the level of effective demand and hence to the overall level of economic activity and employment. What this highlighted was the possibility that an increase in the degree of monopoly, and hence the profit mark-up, without any offsetting increases in investment activity, resulted in economic stagnation or depression – that is, a state of economic activity of less than full employment. The micro-grounding of economic stagnation was developed by Kalecki's friend and colleague, Josef Steindl in his book, *Maturity and Stagnation in American Capitalism* (1952).[1]

By 1950, most of the foundational components of Post Keynesian economics had been developed; but they were not brought together. Instead four separate but compatible lines of inquiry and discussion emerged that twenty years later culminated in the emergence of Post Keynesian economics in 1971. The *first* of these is associated with Joan Robinson and her colleagues at the University of Cambridge, England. Utilizing Kaleckian models, Robinson extended Keynes's arguments about effective demand and economic activity to economic growth. The consequence of this work was the development of a macroeconomic theory of economic activity and economic growth that was significantly different from that being developed by neoclassical economists. The work also reinforced the Kalecki–Steindl argument that the relationship between pricing, the profit mark-up, and investment was the linchpin to understanding the growth and stagnation of economic activity in a capitalist economy. Various economists in a *second* line of inquiry examined this relationship in detail. Robinson's approach to linking pricing, the profit mark-up, and investment emphasized structural relationships, minimized the role of the enterprise and ignored the role of finance in determining the profit mark-up. In contrast, her colleague, Nicholas Kaldor, placed more emphasis on both these factors. Alfred Eichner, Adrian Wood, and Geoff Harcourt argued that the large business enterprise utilized its market power to determine directly its profit mark-up in order to generate the profits needed to finance its investment projects. Finally, Paul Baran, Paul Sweezy, and the monopoly capital school argued that the growth of the profit mark-up was not being offset by increases in private investment and public expenditure. Their contribution to the inquiry was to associate the issue with the behavior of the large business enterprise, to raise the question of what form the increased investment and public expenditure should take, and to emphasize that the relationship between the business community and the state needed to be understood.

A *third* line of research centered on developments in microeconomics. In particular, Philip Andrews (University of Oxford) and Gardiner Means developed complementary non-neoclassical arguments about cost, how enterprises behaved and set their administered prices, and the impact of these administered prices on inflation and the economy.[2] Other economists then extended and developed their arguments: Harry Edwards and Paolo Sylos-Labini argued that barriers to entry based on goodwill, economies to scale, and differential cost advantage enabled enterprises to increase the profit mark-up they could add to their price; other contributions included the modeling of role of the administered price in the reproduction of the enterprise over time by Wilford Eiteman, the delineation of the role of social rules and restrictive trade practices for the control of market competition by George Richardson and Romney Robinson, and the role of leadership in the managing and directing of the business enterprise by Edwin Nourse, Abraham Kaplan, and Alfred Chandler. Another development in microeconomics was the introduction of a multi-industry, circular production input–output model of the economy. Introduced by Piero Sraffa (University of Cambridge), the model provided a mechanism by which pricing and output decisions could be examined simultaneously at the level of the individual enterprise and the economy as a whole. The *fourth* and last line of research dealt with uncertainty and money. Although these issues were extremely important to Keynes himself, they elicited relatively few comments and no systematic development. Dudley Dillard delineated and enlarged Keynes's concept of a monetary economy, while Hyman Minsky was developing his financial instability hypothesis and Paul Davidson worked on understanding Keynes's financial motive and the role of money in the *General Theory*.[3]

Each of the lines of research confirmed to the economists involved (and to those who followed) that there was something seriously wrong with neoclassical economics – wrong in the sense that the theory was wrong. But in most cases they did not think in terms of completely rejecting neoclassical theory and substituting something in its place. However, various social and political issues emerged from the 1950s onwards pushed economists to think more radically. In the United States, they included the anticommunist crusade combined with Khruschev's 1956 speech detailing Stalin's atrocities that had the unintended consequence of opening new ways of thinking about Marxism. In addition there was the civil rights movement, nuclear disarmament, Vietnam War and US imperialism, and the social ills of poverty, discrimination, illiteracy, and the ghetto among others. In the UK it was also the revealing of Stalin's atrocities as well as the Hungarian uprising, the Suez crisis, Rhodesia, South Africa and white rule, Northern Ireland, and government policies that attacked workers, trade unions, and socialism. The response in both countries was the rise of the New Left and the student movement, which in turn prompted interest in Marxism and other alternative ways of economic thinking. It also impressed upon many students and younger economists that neoclassical economic theory could not or simply did not deal with what they viewed were important economic issues – in short neoclassical economics was seen as mostly irrelevant to their concerns.

At the same time there emerged among American and British economists an awareness that economics was in crisis. One view sought the origin of the crisis in the abstract and unrealistic nature of the rapidly evolving, mathematical neoclassical theory that was incapable of answering important economic policy questions. A variant of this view was the concern that the increasingly abstract economic theory was losing its grounding in the real world because its assumptions lacked empirical validity. This concern was increasing because economists seem uninterested in developing new empirical data designed to validate their assumptions and enrich their understanding of the workings of the economy. A second view of the crisis focused on the theoretical inadequacy of the Keynesian neoclassical synthesis to account for inflation and more generally stagflation. This perceived inadequacy provided room for heretical forms of neoclassical theory, that is monetarism, to challenge the theoretical and policy *status quo*. This challenge was interpreted by many as a crisis *qua* counter-revolution; and the solution was a more logically coherent neoclassical theory. For neoclassical economists the crisis was an internal issue: neoclassical economics, although generally sound, had some problems that needed ironing out. Thus, there was no loss of faith in the theory or in the capability of economists to use the theory to discuss, analyze, and resolve important policy issues. However, for others who were influenced by Robinson, Means, Andrews, Kalecki, and Keynes, as well as the capital controversy (which revealed that important aspects of aggregate neoclassical theory were logically incoherent), the crisis arose precisely because of a loss of faith in neoclassical economic theory.

Nevertheless, even these economists who questioned neoclassical economics and thought much of it was useless and irrelevant were not quick to explicitly reject it entirely and develop a non-neoclassical economics in its place. It was easier for them to argue that neoclassical economics was irrelevant or "rubbish"; however, it was much harder for them to break with it entirely and develop an alternative. The break was not only with the theory; it was also with the societal body of economists.

That some economists could contemplate such a break implies that the crisis in economics went far deeper than the problems with theory would suggest. In particular, neoclassical economics in the United States and Britain collectively faced in the 1960s a challenge from alternative theories with their own institutional arrangements. In the United States the first challenge came in 1965 in the form of Institutional economics and the Association for Evolutionary Economics (AFEE), the second in 1968 from radical economics and the Union for Radical Political Economics (URPE), and the third in 1970 from social economics and the Association for Social Economics (ASE). In Britain, the challenge to neoclassical economics came in 1970 from socialist economics and the Conference of Socialist Economists (CSE). In 1971 neoclassical economics faced a new challenger who was primarily interested in repudiating neoclassical theory *per se* and creating an alternative – that challenger was Post Keynesian economics.

THE HISTORY OF POST KEYNESIAN ECONOMICS, 1971–2000[4]

Throughout the 1960s Joan Robinson made several trips to the United States, lecturing on the capital controversies, methodology, and the shortcomings of neoclassical economics. Her 1971 visit to America was no different. Younger, heterodox-inclined economists and graduate students positively received Robinson. They told her horror stories about being unable to protest against neoclassical economics lest they get denied tenure or lose their financial support. At the same time neoclassical professors would not defend the neoclassical theory they made their students learn.

When Robinson was at Columbia University in November, Alfred Eichner talked with her about this lamentable situation and suggested that a way forward would be to set up a meeting between her and sympathetic economists at the upcoming annual meeting of American economists to discuss a possible program of action. The meeting took place on 28 December 1971 with seventeen economists in attendance. The discussion at the meeting was wide-ranging, but those in attendance all agreed that the major economics journal in the United States, the *American Economic Review*, was closed to heterodox economists and that something should be done about it. Eichner agreed to take this matter up with the American Economic Association, who sponsored the journal. He then used this opportunity to create common ground by means of regular communication between those who attended the meeting for the longer-term project of developing an alternative to neoclassical economics. To this end, Eichner asked them to respond to a series of questions on alternative economic theories, whereupon the replies would be sent to all members of the group. Finally, he asked the members whether they knew of other economists who would be interested in joining this effort to supplant neoclassical economic theory, and, if so, requested them to send their names and addresses to him so that he could add them to the mailing list. These latter two activities by Eichner constituted, in the United States, the beginning of Post Keynesian economics as an identifiable body of theory supported by a network of economists and institutions. To build Post Keynesian economics, Eichner decided in January 1972 to establish a newsletter to inform the participants at the December 1971 meeting as well as subsequent economists who joined the group about its current and forthcoming activities. Next, with the help of URPE, Ed Nell and Eichner arranged sessions at the annual meeting of American economists on Post Keynesian economics as an alternative to neoclassical economics. Later in 1978, Sidney Weintraub and Paul Davidson established the *Journal of Post Keynesian Economics*. At this same time, Davidson realized that for Post Keynesian economics to grow, graduate economic students needed to be trained in Post Keynesian economics. Accordingly, he began to promote the graduate program at Rutgers University as a place to study Post Keynesian economics. Finally, Eichner realized that books on Post Keynesian economics needed to be published if it were going to survive and spread. Hence, in 1979 he established a publishing partnership with M.E. Sharpe, Inc. which resulted in the publication of nineteen books on Post Keynesian economics over the next ten years. As a result of efforts by Eichner, Nell, Weintraub, and Davidson, by 1980 there existed in the United States a community of nearly 300 Post Keynesian economists underpinned by an array of institutional support. Over the next twenty years Post Keynesians continued to promote conferences, to publish books and articles to support new Post Keynesian-oriented journals, and to associate with members of AFEE, URPE, and ASE. The outcome of this continual networking and organizational building, the community of Post Keynesian economists increased to over a thousand members by the year 2000.

The development of Post Keynesian economics in Britain proceeded differently than in the United States. The CSE was established in 1970. It provided an organizational context for the development of a radical alternative to neoclassical economics, and for the next five years there was an intense debate as to whether Marxism or a variant of Post Keynesian economics was the way forward, with Marxism being the eventual favorite. As a result, most of the Post Keynesian-oriented economists left the CSE. In its place there emerged an informal network among Post Keynesians. The establishment of the *Thames Papers in Political Economy* (1974), the *British Review of Economic Issues* (1977), and the *Cambridge Journal of Economics* (1977) helped to reinforce the network by providing publishing outlets for Post Keynesian articles. The *Cambridge Journal* also provided institutional support for the development of Post Keynesian economics at Cambridge.

However, it was not until the mid-1980s that Post Keynesian economics visibly emerged in Britain. In 1983, Philip Arestis converted the *Thames Papers* into a Post Keynesian publishing outlet; and then he struck a deal with the publisher Edward Elgar to get many of the *Thames Papers* published in edited volumes. Five years later in 1988, Arestis and Victoria Chick established the Post Keynesian Economics Study Group, which over the next twelve years held thrice-yearly seminars and numerous conferences. In addition, in 1988 John Pheby started his annual Great Malvern Political Economy Conferences that lasted ten years; and in 1989 he established the *Review of Political Economy*. This flurry of Post Keynesian activity resulted in the creation of an identifiable Post Keynesian community in Britain with a network of about 100 members, numerous publishing outlets, and regular meetings. During the 1990s, the Post Keynesian community was further supported by the CSE, which once again opened its annual conference to Post Keynesian papers, the emergence of Tony Lawson's critical realism workshop at Cambridge in 1994, and lastly in 1999, the emergence of the Association for Heterodox Economics with its yearly conference. So by the year 2000 the British Post Keynesian community had expanded to about 150 members.

History of Post Keynesian Theory
The Post Keynesian economic theory of today is in many ways quite different from what emerged and evolved in the 1970s. From today's perspective Post Keynesian economic theory circa 1975 looks not very different from neoclassical economic theory of the same period. In terms of methodology, it employed static,

ahistorical, maximizing, and equilibrium theorizing and models; and it also utilized unrealistic, non-empirically grounded assumptions in its theorizing and modeling. As for economic theorizing, the neoclassical dichotomy of macro-economics versus microeconomics was accepted, as well as the way neoclassical theory pictured the economy. Considering the last point, for example, Post Keynesians argued that their microeconomics dealt with imperfectly competitive markets with significant monopolistic elements, implying that the notion of perfectly competitive markets versus imperfectly competitive markets, as articulated in neoclassical theory, was the correct theoretical picture of the economy.

The existence of these neoclassical vestiges in Post Keynesian theory was largely due to the fact the different intellectual traditions that were the initial base for Post Keynesian econom-ics were not completely free of neoclassical theorizing them-selves. However, because the theoretical content of the different traditions was somewhat different, their convergence set forces in motion that would over time essentially drive out the neoclassical vestiges. This process was greatly assisted by intellectual traditions associated with radical, social and Institu-tional economics, as well as by critical realism. That is to say, over the last twenty years Post Keynesians have consciously borrowed ideas from, have worked with economists from, and have become involved in the associations of these other traditions. In short, Post Keynesians and the other heterodox economists have embarked upon a synthesis, with the outcome being that Post Keynesian theory has changed significantly from what it was in 1975 to a more coherent and clearly non-neoclassical theory.

POST KEYNESIAN ECONOMIC THEORY[5]

Post Keynesian economics is based on a methodological approach that emphasizes realism, history, and empirically grounded theory. Thus, it begins with delineating the structure of a real capitalist economy. That is, a capitalist economy can be pictured or represented in terms of two overlapping inter-dependencies.

The first interdependency is that, to produce goods and services, it requires goods and services to be used as inputs. Hence, with regard to production, the economy can be represented as an input–output matrix of material goods combined with different types of labor skills to produce an array of goods and services as outputs. Many of the outputs replace the goods and services used up in production (and are called intermediate products) and the rest constitute a physical surplus to be used for consumption, private investment, government usage, and exports.

The second interdependency is between the wages of workers, the profits of enterprises, and the taxes of government and expenditures on consumption, investment, and government goods.

The last interdependency is the overlay of the flow of funds or money accompanying the production and exchange of the goods and services. Together they produce a monetary input–output structure of the economy where in each market transactions are monetary transactions; where a change in price of a good or the method in which a good is produced in any one market will have an indirect or direct impact on the entire economy; and where the amount of private investment, government expenditure on real goods and services, and the excess of exports over imports determines the amount of economic activity, the level of employment, and consumer expenditure.

With this structure in place, Post Keynesians next look at two broad categories of economic organizations. The first category is micro-oriented, hence particular to a set of markets and products, and consists of the business enterprise, private and public market organizations that regulate competition in product and service markets, and the organizations and institutions that regulate the wages of workers. The second is macro-oriented and is spread across markets and products, or is not particular to any market or product. It includes the state and various subsidiary organizations as well as particular financial organizations – that is, those organizations that make decisions about government expenditures and taxation, and the interest rate.

Business enterprise

The business enterprise is seen by Post Keynesians as a specific social organization for coordinating and carrying out economic activities in a manner that mirrors the social relationships in capitalist society and, most importantly, reproduce the capitalist class itself. It consists of an organizational component, a production and cost component, a series of routines that transmit information (such as costs, sales, and prices) and enable the workers and managers to coordinate and carry out their activities, and a management that makes strategic decisions about prices and investment. The organization of the business enterprise is essentially a particular social technique for the production of goods and services. Hierarchical in structure and authoritarian in terms of social control, the organization of the enterprise enables management to make its decisions that, in turn, are carried out by lower management and workers. As a result, if management finds that the existing organization is adversely affecting their competitive and growth capabilities, it will simply adopt a new organizational technique for the enterprise. Hence, in terms of organization and management, there is no inherent constraint on what the enterprise can do. The organization of production is also a technique that consists of technologically (and socially) organized workplaces, such as plants. Because the enterprise exists in historical time, it has both new plants with new technology and low costs and old plants with old technology and high costs. Thus, as its output expands, the enterprise has to bring on line more costly plants. However, because of its overhead costs (that is, the costs of management and depreciation), the average cost of producing a good or service declines. This means that the enterprise is predisposed to sell as much as possible at a given price, for the more it sells the more profits it gets. The combination of declining average costs and the plasticity of its organizational structure means that the enterprise faces no internal constraints on its growth over time. Consequently, it directs its attention to those external factors that can adversely affect its existence and constrain its growth, using two tools especially designed to deal with them – setting prices and investment.

When making decisions, management is motivated by different goals, the most fundamental being the survival and continuation of the enterprise, followed by various strategic goals, such as growth of sales, developing new products, entering new geographical regions or markets, generating dividends for shareholders, and/or attaining political power. Given that the enterprise has an unknown but potentially very long life span, the time period to achieve each of the goals is likely to be different, and management cannot be sure that they can achieve them; the goals are not ends in themselves but are established so as to direct the activities of the enterprise in an uncertain environment. As a result, profits are not an end goal for management, but rather an intermediate objective that facilitates the directing of its desired activities.

Management views price setting and the choice of investment projects as strategic decisions designed to meet their goals. With regard to the former, management utilizes cost-plus pricing procedures that involves first calculating the costs of producing the product and then adding a profit mark-up to set the price. The resulting price remains fixed for a period of time (and many transactions) and does not change when sales increase or decrease. Its two most important properties are its potential, depending on the state of demand, to generate a cash flow for the enterprise that will cover its costs producing the product and generate profits, and its strategic capabilities, such as penetrating markets and altering market shares. Once set, the price is then administered to the market as the enterprise's market price. Turning to investment, management distinguishes between investment projects that are designed to replace broken equipment or maintain the operations of an existing plant, to meet state mandated environmental and safety standards, and to expand capacity, create new products, and expand the enterprise's marketing capabilities. Management generally agrees to fund all the investment projects in the first two categories on the grounds that, if they were not supported, the enterprise's capacity for current production would be severely reduced. Investment projects in the third category, on the other hand, have to be justified either in terms of their contribution to meeting the future demand of the enterprise's existing products or in terms of producing new products for current and novel future demands. In addition, they have to meet a range of financial guidelines ranging from generating a flow of profits that would cover their costs in a given number of years to a minimal rate of return (that is greater than the market interest rate). However, given management's goals, the financial guidelines play a secondary role in investment decisions. Once the investment decision has been made, management then determines whether it can be financed internally from profits or whether external funds will have to be obtained from financial institutions.

Markets and workers

The business enterprise sells its goods and services in markets that include products from other competing enterprises. Market is a term that refers to all the transactions of a specific product; hence the economy consists of as many markets as there are products. Many of the markets cover only transactions between enterprises who are buying and selling intermediate and investment products; while the other markets cover transactions between enterprises, consumers, and government involving consumer products and products required by government. In all markets, the relationship between the market price and market sales is non-existent, and a reduction in the market price by itself will generate little or no increase in market sales. Consequently, price wars reduce the profits of the affected enterprises, since they result in the reduction of the profit mark-up with no offsetting increase in sales. To reduce the possibility of destructive price wars, enterprises form private market organizations, such as cartels and price leadership, or promote government regulation in the guise of regulatory commissions or laws to control competition among the enterprises in the market and ensure that a single market price prevails.

In addition to purchasing intermediate products, enterprises also employ workers to produce their output. Given the unequal social relationship between workers and their employers combined with the fact that workers are human beings, not products, there does not exist a labor market *per se*. In its place is a pool of workers whom employers can draw upon at their discretion. The enterprise's demand for workers is dependent on present and future expected sales of its products, not on the wage rates it offers. Since the wage rate constitutes a cost to the enterprise that it attempts to control to maintain its cost competitiveness and the livelihood of workers, a complex set of organizations and institutions exists – for example, employer associations, trade unions, minimum wage legislation, and customary practice – to regulate the wage rate offered to workers and which they are compelled to take. Thus, the wage rate is a social artifact that is designed only to meet the cost-competitiveness demands of enterprises, while maintaining a living, and perhaps contented, workforce.

Government and Finance

Given the above discussion, the economy as a whole can be represented as a series of interrelated product markets, complete with enterprises, prices, quantities and pools of differently skilled workers. Since market prices and market sales are not functionally related, prices do not coordinate or affect the amount of economic activity. Rather, they are designed to generate a cash flow that enables the enterprise to survive and grow. In contrast, investment decisions of enterprises not only direct and coordinate their own activities, they also, individually and in aggregate, help coordinate the economic activity of the economy as a whole and determine the aggregate level of economic activity. However, enterprises' propensities to invest are generally not sufficient to ensure that the level of aggregate economic activity is consistent with full employment. There are two reasons for this: first, the lack of acceptable projects due to insufficient demand or possibly high interest rates and, secondly, insufficient retained profits to fund the investment projects.

Private and public financial institutions help enterprises overcome their insufficient retained profits, thus enabling them to implement and complete a greater number of investment projects. In this manner, financial institutions help promote the propensity of enterprises to invest. Even with the help of financial institutions, however, enterprises still do not undertake enough investment projects to produce full employment.

This persistent tendency towards stagnation in the economy is due to insufficient demand or to the rate of interest; and it can only be overcome by activities undertaken by an extra-market organization, that is the state. Government action through its monetary institutions, such as the Federal Reserve System, can adjust the interest rate in an effort to encourage enterprises to undertake more investment projects and to permit consumers to increase their consumption expenditures. However, given the small role the interest rate plays in management decisions regarding investment projects, its stimulative impact is minimal, especially relative to the impact of a change in the interest rate on consumer expenditures. Complementing its monetary action with fiscal and acting through its legislative bodies, the government can alter various tax rates, such as sales taxes, income taxes, and profit taxes, to increase the after-tax profits of enterprises and the after-tax incomes of consumers, with the expectations that the increased incomes will lead to greater investment expenditures by enterprises and greater consumer expenditures by consumers.

Neither of these activities is, however, capable of generating enough investment and consumer expenditures to push the economy towards full employment. What is also required is government expenditures on social, infrastructure, or any other programs. These expenditures increase the demand for public employees (who then spend their wages on the products of private enterprise) as well as direct demand for the products of private enterprise. As a result, government expenditures increase the aggregate demand in the economy and have the potential to drive the economy towards full employment. Whether a government in a capitalist economy has the latitude to adopt such a policy depends on its relationship to the business community, to the capitalist class in general, and to the working class.

POST KEYNESIANISM AND CAPITALISM[6]

The twofold picture of capitalism that emerges from Post Keynesian theory is one of inherent chronic stagnation at the macro-level and one of control and dominance by the business enterprise and business community at the micro-level. Because many Post Keynesians have a liberal view of capitalism, they retain an ameliorative attitude towards it. Consequently, they ignore the micro and focus their attention on the macro picture and the problem of stagnation. Their attention to the macro is also due to the fact that, since prices and wage rates do not coordinate or affect the amount of economic activity, state policies designed to reduce them, such as increasing the degree of competition among business enterprises by enforcing anti-trust laws and passing anti-trade union legislation, would have little impact on increasing economic activity. The more conservative liberal Post Keynesian argues that the state should pursue some kind of fiscal and monetary policies to push the economy towards full employment; but, as noted above, such policies cannot really do the job. Hence, the more progressive liberal Post Keynesian argues that the state must engage in direct expenditures on social, infrastructure, or other programs.

One policy proposal in this vein, which draws on Institution-alist, Marxian, and other heterodox traditions as well as proposals by Hyman Minsky (1986) for a permanent Works Progress Administration-style program, argues that the government should act as an employer of last resort (ELR) by guaranteeing jobs for all. The employment program is managed by a functional finance approach to budgetary matters, with government deficits seen as necessary for overcoming the propensity of business enterprises and the rich not to spend all of their profits and income. It is based on a Chartalist's view of modern money that says money or currency is the creature of the state, a position that is compatible with Post Keynesian theory. As a result, neither taxes nor bond sales are necessary to finance government spending; instead, government income, sales and profit taxes create a demand for the state currency. Consequently, the state only has to create, that is print, the money that it then pays to its ELR employees.

There are several versions of the ELR policy proposal. In most, access to the ELR program is open to all with no means tests or time limits; workers are paid a near minimum wage, but get health care benefits; and workers are engaged in service jobs that contribute to the community, such as environmental clean-up, parks and recreation, and care for the elderly. In addition, it is possible to view the program as a vehicle for progressive social policies in that the government ELR job becomes a "benchmark" for the private sector, as any worker has the option of taking the ELR job. Thus, business enterprises will have to match the wage-benefits package and work environments of the ELR job (or compensate in some other way, such as opportunity for career advancement) or risk losing workers to the government. As a result, some Post Keynesians see the program as a means by which the state can pressure the private sector to increase wages and offer health benefits. On the other hand, business enterprises also benefit, as they now have the option of hiring out of the ELR pool of workers rather than out of the general pool of unemployed, many of whom they consider unemployable. Hence the program can also be seen as "employing the reserve army," as the ELR pool now takes the place of the traditional reserve army, expanding (contracting) when the private sector contracts (expands). Finally, some of the more radical Post Keynesians view the program as a possible way of valuing activities not endorsed by the market. Arts and music, community gardens, and other activities may qualify as ELR jobs.

This, almost blind, reliance on the state to adopt progressive economic policies is, however, questionable. What liberal Post Keynesians ignore is that the actions of the state are subject to pressures by various interest groups, including the business community. Thus, when proposing such programs as above, Post Keynesians fail to inquire whether they are in the interest of those groups who determine government policies. For example, Michael Kalecki argued many years ago that, if the state pursued a full employment policy, the initial result would be that workers would gain significant workplace control that would then be followed by the business community pushing for increased unemployment so as to regain control over the workplace. The importance of the scenario is that the state responds to interest group pressures and that the business community is a powerful interest group whose voice is often or predominately heard. However, if the complete macro–micro picture of capitalism is embraced, a more radical view of capitalism can be drawn from Post Keynesian economic theory.

That is to say, the ameliorative economic proposals advocated by liberal Post Keynesians for the problem of stagnation do not deal directly with the control and dominance micro-issues of capitalism, such as the conditions of work and the control of laboring activities, who it is determines what is produced and how it is produced, and who decides on the division of the physical surplus among enterprises, management, workers, and government activities that also contribute to the problem.

Since government expenditures are necessary to push the economy towards full employment, the question is: in a capitalist economy, is it in the interest of the business community and the capitalist class to promote economic policies that lead to full employment? As noted by Kalecki, the push towards full employment would mean that business enterprises would begin to lose their managerial-authoritarian control over workers. It would mean the loss of control, not simply as represented, say, by demands for higher wages and better benefits, but also over the production process itself as well as over its exclusive power to make the pricing, investment, and wage–salary–dividend decisions. That is to say, in a full-employment economy, workers can strike and change jobs with impunity. Hence they are in the position to negotiate for more control over their working lives including changes in management structure and authority, for input into the pricing and investment decisions, and for changes in the wage-salary structure and in the payment of dividends. Since capitalism is based on the absolute control of workers by management and the business community, any weakening of this relationship is not in their long-term interest. So, in spite of the greater profits that come with a fully employed capitalist economy, the business community would choose control over profits.

If the general public starts to accept that government expenditures are necessary to promote full employment, then the state could eventually be seen, in contrast to the business community, as the driving force in the economy. Consequently the business community loses stature, legitimacy, and the claim of primacy over the state in directing the economy. As a result, it becomes possible for the state to initiate national economic planning that could oversee, direct, or influence the investment, production and pricing decisions of business enterprises. Moreover, with the increased political power of workers arising from full employment, the direction of the government expenditures could further weaken the business community's control of their workers through creating services that soften the blow of being unemployed or out on strike; could generate a wider array of economic transactions that are not under the control of the business community; and could reallocate the physical surplus between workers and management. To forestall these possibilities, the business community would use its economic and political power to influence government economic policy to be business-friendly by not promoting full employment, by acquiescing to the leading role of the business community, and by promoting government expenditures that are at least non-detrimental, if not actually beneficial to the business community.

The state is not a neutral social organization but one that carries out the interests of the dominant political groups. Consequently, given the dominant political position the business community occupies in a capitalist economy, it is not possible for the state to adopt and maintain full employment economic policies, since to do so would fundamentally alter the relationship between the business community and the workers whom they control. As Joan Robinson noted over sixty years ago:

> In the present age, any government which had both the power and the will to remedy the major defects of the capitalist system would have the will and the power to abolish it altogether, while governments which have the power to retain the system lack the will to remedy its defects.[7]

Many others have also added that those who have power often see what radical Post Keynesians call "defects" as virtues.

To sum up, the complete Post Keynesian macro–micro theory of capitalism portrays the state largely as a servant of the interests of the business community and the capitalist class. The implication that radical Post Keynesians draw from this is that capitalism cannot be made to work better, rather it must be completely changed. What might replace capitalism, however, cannot be deduced from Post Keynesian economic theory or the policies Post Keynesians advocate. Post Keynesian theory only explains how a capitalist economy works; it is not a blueprint for the good society.

NOTES

1. For further readings about these contributions, see Sawyer (1985), Hamouda and Harcourt (1988), Lee and Samuels (1992), and Lee (1998).
2. At the same time, they explicitly stated that many neoclassical concepts, such as enterprise demand curves, increasing marginal costs, U-shaped average total cost curves, enterprise equilibrium, and maximization, had no empirical or theoretical support and hence were completely rejected.
3. For further readings, see Lee (1998), Robinson (1956), Baran and Sweezy (1966), Minsky (1982), and Davidson (1972).
4. For further readings, see King (2002) and Lee (1998 and 2000).
5. For further readings on Post Keynesian economic theory, see Eichner (1987), Dow (1991), Lavoie (1992), Davidson (1994), Arestis (1996), and Lee (1998).
6. For further readings, see Minsky (1986), Warner, Forstater, and Rosen (2000), and Kalecki (1943).
7. Robinson (1936, p. 693).

REFERENCES

Arestis, P. (1996) "Post-Keynesian Economics: Towards Coherence," *Cambridge Journal of Economics* 20.1 (January): 111–35.

Baran, P. and Sweezy, P. (1966) *Monopoly Capital: An Essay on the American Economic and Social Order*. New York: Monthly Review Press.

Davidson, P. (1972) *Money and the Real World*. New York: John Wiley and Sons.

Davidson, P. (1994) *Post Keynesian Macroeconomics Theory*. Aldershot: Edward Elgar.

Dillard, D. (1948) *The Economics of John Maynard Keynes: The Theory of a Monetary Economy*, Englewood Cliffs: Prentice-Hall.

Dow, S. (1991) "The Post-Keynesian School." In D. Mair and A. Miller, eds, *A Modern Guide to Economic Thought: An Introduction to Comparative Schools of Thought in Economics*, pp. 176–206. Aldershot: Edward Elgar.

Eichner, A. (1987) *The Macrodynamics of Advanced Market Economies*. Armonk: M.E. Sharpe, Inc.

Hamouda, O.F. and Harcourt, G.C. (1988) "Post Keynesianism: From Criticism to Coherence?," *Bulletin of Economic Research* 40 (January): 1–33.

Kalecki, M. (1943) "Political Aspects of Full Employment," *Political Quarterly* 14.4: 322–31.

Keynes, J. M. (1936) *The General Theory of Employment, Interest and Money*. New York: Harcourt, Brace and Company.

King, J. (2002) *A History of Post Keynesian Macroeconomics, 1936–2000*. Aldershot: Edward Elgar.

Lavoie, M. (1992) *Foundations of Post-Keynesian Economic Analysis*. Aldershot: Edward Elgar.

Lee, F. (1998) *Post Keynesian Price Theory*. Cambridge: Cambridge University Press.

Lee, F. (2000) "The Organizational History of Post Keynesian Economics in America, 1971–1995," *Journal of Post Keynesian Economics* 23 (Fall): 141–62.

Lee, F. and Samuels, W. (eds) (1992) *The Heterodox Economics of Gardiner C. Means: A Collection*. Armonk: M.E. Sharpe.

Minsky, H. (1982) *Can It Happen Again?*. Armonk: M.E. Sharpe.

Minsky, H. (1986) *Stabilizing an Unstable Economy*. New Haven: Yale University Press.

Robinson, J. (1936) Review of *The Trade Cycle* by R.F. Harrod. *The Economic Journal* 46 (December): 691–3.

Robinson, J. (1956) *The Accumulation of Capital*. London: The Macmillan Press Ltd.

Sawyer, M. (1985) *The Economics of Michael Kalecki*. London: Macmillan.

Steindl, J. (1952) *Maturity and Stagnation in American Capitalism*. Oxford: Basil Blackwell.

Warner, A., Forstater, M., and Rosen, S. (2000) *Commitment to Full Employment*. Armonk: M.E. Sharpe.

6   PAUL SWEEZY AND
MONOPOLY CAPITAL

John Bellamy Foster

We live at a time when capitalism has become more extreme, and is more than ever presenting itself as a force of nature, which demands such extremes. Globalization – the spread of the self-regulating market to every niche and cranny of the globe – is portrayed by its mainly establishment proponents as a process that is unfolding from everywhere at once with no center and no discernible power structure. As the *New York Times* claimed in its July 7, 2001 issue, repeating now fashionable notions, today's global reality is one of "a fluid, infinitely expanding and highly organized system that encompasses the world's entire population," but which lacks any privileged positions or "place of power."[1]

Even the revolutionary figure of Karl Marx has been enlisted in support of this view of inexorable global destiny, which seemingly determines everything, but which has no manifest agent of change. Thus the World Bank quoted from *The Communist Manifesto* by Marx and Engels on the opening page of its 1996 World Development Report, arguing that the transition from planned to market economies and the entire thrust of neoliberal globalization was an inescapable, elemental process, lacking any visible hand behind it:

> Constant revolutionizing of production, uninterrupted disturbance of social conditions, everlasting uncertainty and agitation … All fixed, fast frozen relations, with their train of ancient and venerable prejudices, and opinions, are swept away, all new-formed ones become antiquated before they can ossify. All that is solid melts into air …

Gone – spirited away by ellipses in the World Bank quotation from the *Manifesto* – were Marx and Engels' allusions in the same passage to "the bourgeois epoch" and their subsequent reference to how "the need for a constantly expanding market for its products chases the bourgeoisie over the whole surface of the globe."

It is no doubt largely in response to this atmosphere of inevitability, in which globalization is divorced from all agency, that the movement against the neoliberal global project has chosen to exaggerate the role of the visible instruments of globalization at the expense of any serious consideration of historical capitalism. Radical dissenters frequently single out the WTO, the IMF, the World Bank and multinational corporations – and even specific corporations like McDonald's – for criticism, while deemphasizing the system, and its seemingly inexorable forces.

These two distorted viewpoints, one generally in support of globalization, the other generally opposed, are mutually reinforcing in their unreality. Those who wish to intervene in these processes are thus left with no real material basis on which to ground their actions. Both perspectives have in common an emphasis on the decline of nation state sovereignty. Adam Smith described capitalism in the late eighteenth century as a system that eliminated all need for a sovereign power in the economic realm, replacing the visible hand of the absolutist or mercantilist state with the invisible hand of the market."The Sovereign," he wrote, "is completely discharged from a duty" with respect to the market (Book 4, section 9). Now we are told that this invisible hand has been globalized to such an extent that the sovereign power of nation states over their territorial domains themselves has been vastly diminished. For *New York Times* foreign affairs columnist Thomas Friedman, author of *The Lexus and the Olive Tree*, globalization is a new technological-economic system based in the microchip and ruled by an "electronic herd" of financial investors and multinational corporations, free from any nation state or power structure, and beholden to none.

Those seeking to dispel such views might reply that capitalism with all of its contradictions remains, but most current conceptions of capitalism are too lacking in historical specificity and concreteness, and too wrapped up in the notion of unfettered competition, to be useful in countering this dominant ideology. Indeed, the very idea of capitalism is being shorn of all determinate elements. The notion of global free market hegemony without the nation-state and without discernible centers of power (only highly visible instruments of the market) means a concept of capitalism that has become virtually synonymous with globalization. There is, it is proclaimed, no alternative because there is nothing outside the system, and no center within the system.

The ideological fog that pervades all aspects of the globalization debate is bound to dissipate eventually, as it becomes clear that the contradictions of capitalism, which have never been surmounted, are present in more universal and more destructive form than ever before. For those seeking to penetrate this fog at present and to understand the constellation of forces in the world today what is needed above all is a concrete and historically specific conception of capitalism that will allow us to see through such issues as globalization. Within Marxism such an analysis was provided in the twentieth century by the theory of monopoly capitalism.

THE ORIGINS OF MONOPOLY CAPITAL THEORY

The term "monopoly capitalism" has been widely used within Marxian economics to refer to the stage of capitalism dominated by large corporations. This stage of capitalist development originated in the last quarter of the nineteenth century and reached maturity about the time of the Second World War. Marx's *Capital*, like the work of the other classical political economists, had assumed that the market system was characterized by conditions of free competition, in which capitalist enterprises were small, mainly family-run firms. Classical political economy never included such absolute fantasies as "perfect" or "pure" competition, which were to be imported into economics in its later neoclassical stage. Nevertheless, it assumed in its bedrock theory of free competition that price competition was fierce, and that no individual capitalist or firm had the power to control a significant portion of the market.[2]

In the case of Marx, as distinct from the other classical political economists, however, capitalism was a historical system, and thus dynamic in character, passing through various stages. Although Marx himself did not present a theory of monopoly capitalism, he did point to the concentration and centralization of capital as a fundamental tendency of accumulation under capitalism. The whole development of the credit system and the stock market was for Marx "a new and terrible weapon in the battle of competition and is finally transformed into an enormous social mechanism for the centralization of capitals" (Volume 1, chapter 2, section 2). In preparing Volumes 2 and 3 of Marx's *Capital* for publication two decades later, Engels emphasized the fact that free competition had reached "the end of its road" (Volume 3, chapter 27). Marx and Engels, however, were prone to see these developments as signs of new conditions of socialization of production that would help usher in a new mode of production – not as indications of a new stage of capitalism.

It remained for later thinkers, therefore, to analyze what these developments meant for capitalism's laws of motion. The first to do so was the heterodox U.S. economist Thorstein Veblen who, in *The Theory of Business Enterprise* (1904) and subsequent works, charted the economic implications of the rise of big business, and the transformations in credit, corporate finance and the forms of salesmanship that went along with this. But Veblen's influence on economics did not extend beyond the United States. Within the Marxist tradition, then centered in Germany, the first important theorist of monopoly capitalism was the Austrian economist Rudolf Hilferding in his *Finance Capital: The Latest Phase of Capitalism* (1910); soon followed by Lenin in his *Imperialism: The Highest Stage of Capitalism* (1916).

Hilferding pointed to the tendency of concentration and centralization of capital to generate a greater and greater consolidation of capital, pointing eventually to one big cartel – an overly simplistic view that failed to perceive some of the countervailing influences at work. He saw these changes as mainly quantitative in character and, though his work was full of important insights, he did not explore the question of qualitative alterations in the laws of motion of capitalism. Hilferding's perspective did, however, inspire Lenin to connect imperialism with the monopoly stage of capitalism, and to perceive the growth of giant capital therefore as integrally related to both the expansion of capital on the world stage, and the struggle between nation-states for shares of the world market. Lenin, however, like Hilferding before him, did not pursue the question of how capitalism's basic laws of motion might be modified in the monopoly stage. The concept of monopoly capitalism was to remain axiomatic for Soviet economists in the 1920s and 1930s, during which some important new departures were begun. But by the late 1930s it had been reduced to a mere dogma within the rigid orthodoxy that prevailed under Stalinism.

In the 1930s in the West, meanwhile, mainstream academic economists finally began to deal with monopoly, particularly in the work of Joan Robinson, Edward Chamberlain and the young Paul Sweezy. Yet the theory of "imperfect competition" that was to emerge from these analyses had a formal character that was usually divorced from real historical processes. Nor was it intended as more than a minor qualification to the theory of perfect competition, which continued to be considered the general rule, and prevailed over economics as a whole.

By the 1930s Marxian economics could be said to have three strands: (1) the theory of capital accumulation and crisis; (2) the beginnings of a theory of monopoly capitalism (based on Marx's concept of the concentration and centralization of capital); and (3) the theory of imperialism. The second and third strands – growing monopolization and imperialism – had been linked to each other by Lenin. However, paradoxically, there was no theoretical analysis that linked the second strand to the first – that is, no connection was drawn between growing concentration and centralization of capital and the forms of accumulation and crisis. The debate on economic crisis in Marxian theory, which in the early twentieth century centered on Marx's famous reproduction schemes in in *Capital*, Volume 2, took place in a context that was completely separate from the analysis of the growth of monopoly.

Historical developments, however, were pointing to such a connection. Since the turn of the century in the United States there had been a groundswell of popular agitation against the giant monopolies and trusts. The great merger wave at the beginning of the twentieth century was widely viewed as representing a qualitatively new reality. It has been estimated that between a quarter and a third of all U.S. capital assets underwent consolidation in mergers between 1898 and 1902 alone. The mammoth merger of the period, the formation of U.S. Steel in 1901 under the financial guidance of the investment banking house of Morgan, fused 165 separate companies. The result was a monopolistic corporation controlling about 60 per cent of the total U.S. steel industry. In 1936, Arthur R. Burns wrote his classic study, *The Decline of Competition: A Study of the Evolution of American Industry*. In the context of the Great Depression of the 1930s it was frequently contended within heterodox economic circles, especially among those influenced by Veblen, that the stagnation was worsened by the growth of giant corporations with a large degree of monopoly power. One of the objects of the Temporary National Economic Committee established by the Roosevelt administration during the Great Depression was to investigate this question (though the results that they came up with in the end were quite meager).

Yet, despite all of this, John Maynard Keynes' *General Theory of Employment, Interest and Money* (1936), which transformed macroeconomics in response to the Depression, remained rooted in the age-old assumptions of atomistic competition.

The first economist to connect the theory of crisis to the theory of monopoly was the Polish economist Michal Kalecki, who drew his inspiration from Marx and Rosa Luxemburg. Kalecki's work in the early 1930s in Polish had developed, according to Joan Robinson and others in the circle of younger economists around Keynes, the main elements of the "Keynesian" revolution, in anticipation of Keynes himself. Kalecki moved to England in the mid-1930s where he helped further the transformation in economic analysis associated with Keynes. There he developed his concept of the "degree of monopoly," which stood for the extent to which a firm was able to impose a price mark-up on prime production costs (workers' wages and raw materials). In this way, Kalecki was able to link monopoly power to the distribution of national income, and to the sources of economic crisis and stagnation. Kalecki also explored the more general historical conditions affecting investment. In the closing paragraphs of his *Theory of Economic Dynamics* (1965) he concluded: "Long-run development is not inherent in the capitalist economy. Thus specific 'developmental factors' are required to sustain a long-run upward movement."

This analysis was carried forward by Josef Steindl, a young Austrian economist who had worked closely with Kalecki in England. According to Steindl's *Maturity and Stagnation in American Capitalism* (1952), giant corporations tended to promote widening profit margins, but were constantly threatened by a shortage of effective demand, due to the uneven distribution of income and resulting weakness of wage-based consumption.[3] New investment could conceivably pick up the slack. Yet such investment resulted in new productive capacity, that is, an enlargement of the potential supply of goods. "The tragedy of investment," Kalecki wrote, "is that it is useful."[4] Giant firms, able to control to a considerable extent their levels of price, output, and investment, would not invest if large portions of their existing productive capacity were already standing idle. Confronted with a downward shift in final demand, monopolistic or oligopolistic firms would not lower prices (as in the perfectly competitive system assumed in most economic analysis) but would instead rely almost exclusively on cutbacks in output, capacity utilization and new investment. In this way they would maintain, to whatever extent possible, existing prices and prevailing profit margins. The giant firm under monopoly capitalism was thus prone to wider profit margins (or higher rates of exploitation) and larger amounts of excess capacity than was the case for a freely competitive system, thereby generating a strong tendency toward economic stagnation.[5]

MONOPOLY CAPITAL: AN ESSAY ON THE AMERICAN ECONOMIC AND SOCIAL ORDER

The appearance in 1942 of Paul Sweezy's classic study *The Theory of Capitalist Development*, one of the great works in Marxian economics, marked the beginnings of a distinctive tradition of Marxian analysis within the United States – one that was later to become associated with the magazine *Monthly Review*, which Sweezy founded in 1949 along with historian and journalist Leo Huberman.[6] In *The Theory of Capitalist Development*, Sweezy drew on Marx's theory of realization crisis – showing the close connection between that and Keynes' theory of effective demand – and developed a sophisticated analysis of economic stagnation. *The Theory of Capitalist Development* also extended the Marxian analysis of monopolization. But these two elements remained separate in his work. It was this criticism that Steindl presented in a long discussion of Sweezy's book in *Maturity and Stagnation in American Capitalism*. Steindl went on to argue that a more unified theory could "be organically developed out of ... Marx" based on Kalecki's model of capitalist dynamics, which had connected the phenomenon of realization crisis to the increasing "degree of monopoly" in the economy as a whole.

Sweezy was immediately impressed by Steindl's argument, as was Paul Baran, professor of economics at Stanford, and a close friend and associate of Sweezy and *Monthly Review*. In 1957, Baran published *The Political Economy of Growth*, which adapted the theory of monopoly capitalism arising from Kalecki and Steindl, while also analyzing the role of imperialism in reinforcing the economic underdevelopment of countries in capitalism's third world periphery.[7]

With respect to the latter part of his argument, Baran made a big departure from orthodox economics. Rather than following the common practice of assuming that the poorer economies of the periphery had always been relatively "backward," Baran approached the issue historically. "The question that immediately arises," he wrote, "is why is it that in the backward countries there has been no advance along the lines of capitalist development that are familiar from the history of other capitalist countries, and why is it that forward movement there has been either slow or altogether absent" (*Political Economy of Growth*, p. 136). The answer, he suggested, was to be found in the way in which capitalism was brought to these regions during the period of what Marx called "primitive accumulation," characterized by "undisguised looting, enslavement and murder," and in the way in which this very process has served to "smother fledgling industries" in the colonized societies (ibid., p. 142).

It was thus the European conquest and plundering of the rest of the globe that generated the great divide between the core and periphery of the capitalist world economy that persists to this day. In illustrating this, Baran highlighted the different ways in which India and Japan were incorporated into the world economy as a result of the globalizing tendencies of capitalism: the first as a dependent social formation carrying the unfortunate legacy of what Andre Gunder Frank was later to call "the development of underdevelopment"; the second representing the exceptional case of a society that was neither colonized nor subject for long to unequal treaties, and that, retaining control over its own economic surplus, was free to develop along the autocentric lines of the core European powers. The implication of this analysis was clear: incorporation on an unequal basis into the periphery of the capitalist world economy is itself the main cause of the plight of the underdeveloped countries.

For Baran, imperialism, in this sense, was inseparable from capitalism. Its central underpinnings were to be found in the mode of accumulation operating in the advanced capitalist world. An international division of labor had evolved that geared production and trade of the poor countries in the periphery much more toward the needs of the rich countries in the center of the system than to the needs of their own populations.

No treatment of contemporary imperialism was complete, however, that did not take account of the laws of motion of monopoly capital. In *The Political Economy of Growth*, Baran applied the concept of economic surplus to analyze not only the development of underdevelopment in the periphery, but also to throw light on the problem of accumulation and stagnation within the United States and other leading capitalist nations. This argument was further extended in *Monopoly Capital: An Essay on the American Economic and Social Order*, coauthored with Paul Sweezy, and published in 1966, two years after Baran's death. Between 1966 and 1974 *Monopoly Capital* was translated into sixteen languages and was "adopted ... almost immediately as a standard text" of the New Left.[8]

The basic dilemma of accumulation under monopoly capitalism was laid out in Kaleckian terms. Workers, the vast majority of the population in the rich countries, had little or no access to economic surplus in the forms of profit, interest and rent. Workers' income was almost exclusively wage income. Most working people lived from paycheck to paycheck (though sometimes able to make large purchases on credit), and had no savings to speak of. Workers therefore spent what they got on necessities, or what economists sometimes called "wage goods."

Capitalists, in contrast, had access to economic surplus and had as their main goal accumulation of even greater surplus. They spent a small portion of their total income on luxury goods for their private consumption, but mainly sought to ensure the enhancement of their wealth through investment in capital goods – new productive capacity. But here a dilemma entered in: if all investment-seeking surplus was invested in new productive capacity (new plant and equipment), that new capacity, once it came on stream, would result in a total capacity to produce goods that might well exceed final demand, leading to overproduction, declining prices and rapidly falling profits. In order to prevent such a situation from developing and in order to prevent price reductions that would threaten profit margins, monopoly capital held down production levels, increasing the normal amount of idle productive capacity and carefully regulating investment. Yet all of this meant that the surplus that the system was actually and potentially capable of producing normally exceeded the capacity to absorb that surplus. The result was a trend rate of economic growth well below the potential.

Monopolization, this theory argued, was not the only historical element serving to slow down capital accumulation. Also important was the phenomenon of "maturity" emphasized by Keynes' leading U.S. follower Alvin Hansen during the debates on secular stagnation in the 1930s. Investment, in this perspective, had to be viewed historically. Most new industries went through a highly competitive shakedown phase in which prices tended to fall and investment took a highly dynamic character. However, once such industries had "matured," with more productive capacity built-up than they could normally utilize – and once these industries had also fallen under the sway of three or four monopolistic or oligopolistic firms – investment tended to fall off. What investment took place was more and more supplied out of depreciation funds with relatively little new net investment taking place. Moreover, the nature of industrialization was such that in the highly developed economies a larger and larger portion of industry would consist of mature markets in this sense.

The overall theory thus suggested that the stagnation that had characterized the 1930s was not simply an anomaly, but reflected conditions deeply embedded in the laws of motion of capitalism in its monopoly stage. Nonetheless, the immediate reality at the time that *Monopoly Capital* was written was not stagnation but rapid economic growth. As Baran and Sweezy wrote in the introduction to their book: "The Great Depression of the 1930's accorded admirably with Marxian theory, and its occurrence of course strengthened the belief that similar catastrophic economic breakdowns were inevitable in the future. And yet, much to the surprise of many Marxists, two decades have passed since the end of the Second World War without the recurrence of severe depression" [*Monopoly Capital*, p. 3].

If a monopoly capitalist economy was prone to economic crisis and stagnation, how had the U.S. economy managed to expand for two decades without a major crisis? This was the question that *Monopoly Capital* sought above all to answer. Baran and Sweezy singled out a number of countervailing factors that had served to prop up the economy: (1) the epoch-making stimulus provided in the 1950s by a second great wave of automobilization in the United States (which was to be understood as also encompassing the expansion of the steel, glass, rubber and petroleum industries, the building of the interstate highway systems and the stimulus provided by suburbanization); (2) Cold War military spending, including two regional wars in Asia; (3) the growing wasteful penetration of the sales effort into production (a point first emphasized by Veblen); and (4) the vast expansion of financial superstructure of the capitalist economy, to the extent that it even began to dwarf production itself. (This last element was mentioned in Baran and Sweezy's analysis, but given much more emphasis in Sweezy's later writings than in *Monopoly Capital* itself.) Through these means the U.S. economy managed to absorb surplus and thus to stave off a severe economic crisis.

All of these countervailing factors, however, were either self-limiting, or produced additional contradictions for monopoly capitalist society. Automobilization represented a shift in the entire geographical basis of the economy; and once these effects had been achieved the process slowed down. Moreover, no new epoch-making innovation on the same scale seemed to be on the horizon – even the digital revolution in recent decades has been small in comparison, in its effect on overall investment. The emphasis on military spending committed the United States, which now accounts for roughly a third of all military spending in the world, to global militarism and imperialism – and to the search for new justifications for a large and expanding arms budget once the Cold War had ended. The penetration of the sales effort into the production process meant the production of huge amounts of waste (unnecessary packaging, useless products, throwaway goods and product obsolescence within the process of production itself). Naturally, this was not without its effects on business costs and competition. The skyrocketing growth of the financial superstructure of the capitalist economy at the same time as the relative stagnation of its productive base could only contribute to the uncertainty and instability of capitalist economies worldwide.

Monopoly Capital dealt with the changing nature of competition, the modifications in accumulation, and the growing militarism and imperialism under monopoly capitalism. It largely ignored, however, a question at the heart of Marx's critique of capitalism: the labor process itself, and the exploitation of workers. This topic was taken up Harry Braverman, director of Monthly Review Press – a former skilled worker in metal working industries – in his magnum opus, *Labor and Monopoly Capital: The Degradation of Work in the Twentieth Century* (1974). Braverman, while rooting his analysis in Marx's *Capital*, applied this to the growth of scientific management or Taylorism, which had emerged along with the giant corporation at the beginning of the twentieth century. He showed that the forces directed at the extraction of ever greater amounts of surplus from the direct producers by means of the relentless division and subdivision of labor, and hence the degradation and dehumanization of work, had only intensified under monopoly capitalism. At the same time, the "universalization of the market," to the point that all aspects of social existence became dependent upon it, represented the hidden set of chains behind the much-celebrated growth of "consumer society."[9]

Another extension of the theory of monopoly capitalism was provided in the work of Harry Magdoff – who in 1969, following Leo Huberman's death, became coeditor with Sweezy of *Monthly Review*. Magdoff's *The Age of Imperialism: The Economics of U.S. Foreign Policy* (1969) had as its object nothing less than the rediscovery of the long-suppressed topic of U.S. imperialism. It demonstrated that the U.S. had an empire, although one different from the empires of Britain and France that had preceded it. This, even more than the contest with the Soviet Union, was the context in which the Vietnam War, then taking place, had to be understood. Arguing against the widespread view that the U.S. economy had very little involvement in the world economy, Magdoff emphasized the flow of foreign direct investment abroad and its effect in creating a cumulative stock of investment generating a return flow of earnings. He criticized the common error of simply comparing exports or the foreign investment of multinational corporations to the gross domestic product. Rather, the importance of these economic flows could only be gauged by relating them to strategic sectors of the economy, such as the capital goods industries; or by comparing the earnings on foreign investment to the profits of domestic nonfinancial corporations. Earnings from overseas investments, Magdoff pointed out, had grown from 10 per cent of after tax profits for U.S. nonfinancial corporations in 1950, to over 20 per cent in 1964.[10] In answer to the question "Is Imperialism Necessary?" Magdoff insisted that imperialism was the global face of capitalism – as fundamental to the system as the drive for profits itself.[11]

The formation of the General Agreement on Tariffs and Trade, the International Monetary Fund, and the World Bank after the Second World War facilitated, Magdoff argued, the development of an international order in which the United States assumed a hegemonic position. Already in *The Age of Imperialism* in the late 1960s he emphasized the international financial expansion of U.S. capital, based on the dollar's hegemonic position in the world economy, and the growth at the same time of a debt trap in the Third World. In the closing pages of *The Age of Imperialism*, Magdoff wrote:

> The typical international business firm is no longer limited to the giant oil company. It is as likely to be a General Motors or a General

Electric – with 15 to 20 percent of its operations involved in foreign business, and exercising all efforts to increase this share. It is the professed goal of these international firms to obtain the lowest unit production costs on a world-wide basis. It is also their aim, though not necessarily openly stated, to come out on top in the merger movement in the European Common Market and to control as large a share of the world market as they do of the United States market. (p. 200)

THE NEW STAGE OF GLOBALIZATION

The theory of monopoly capital developed by Sweezy, Baran, Magdoff, and Braverman, on foundations laid by Marx, Veblen, Hilferding, Lenin, Kalecki, and Steindl, thus pointed early on to many of the phenomena that are now commonly associated with "globalization." In this perspective, however, capitalism had been a global system from the start. Although one could refer to a "new stage of globalization," it was part of a long historical process, inseparable from imperialism (Magdoff, *Globalization – To What End?*, p. 3). Capitalism, as Sweezy stressed, had emerged in the fifteenth and sixteenth centuries. From its earliest infancy the system had been constituted as "a dialectical unity of self-directed center and dependent periphery." Further:

> The fact that capitalism has from the beginning had these two poles – which can be variously described by such terms as independent and dependent, dominant and subordinate, developed and underdeveloped, center and periphery – has at every stage been crucial for the evolution of its parts. The driving force has always been the accumulation process in the center, with the peripheral societies being molded by a combination of coercion and market forces to conform to the requirements and serve the needs of the center. (Sweezy, *Four Lectures on Marxism*, p. 73)

Within this global system much higher rates of exploitation were to be found in the periphery than in the center; and at the same time surplus was siphoned off from the periphery to meet the development needs of the center. Consequently, the gap in income and wealth between the center and the periphery as a whole has tended to increase, despite development in some peripheral countries. Conflict between center and periphery was therefore inevitable, oftentimes taking the form of revolution and counterrevolution (the latter invariably supported by the United States and other imperial powers in the center of the system, sometimes through direct military intervention).

The struggle over imperialism, however, did not simply occur between North and South. As Lenin had argued, the growth of monopoly capital was inseparable from rivalry among the advanced industrialized nations within the center of the world system, taking the form of trade and currency conflicts, struggles arising out of the promotion of their respective national corporations, and even leading to war (as in the First and Second World Wars). Much of this imperialist rivalry was directed at spheres of influence and control in the periphery, with each of the great powers laying primary claim to certain dependent regions.

Concentration and centralization of capital, stagnation tendencies in the center, imperialist exploitation in the periphery, globalization of finance, and imperial rivalry between the advanced capitalist countries – together made up the general picture of the world developed by monopoly capital theory. This generated an approach to the latest phase of globalization entirely different from those most commonly encountered today. National sovereignty in the center of the system (as opposed to the periphery), according to the perspective of monopoly capital theory, was not eroded. The world economy was seen neither as chaotic, in the sense of a lack of powerful organizing forces, nor, as some contended, as giving rise to a new international of capital led by the WTO and other supranational organizations. "For the sake of perspective," Magdoff explained in his treatise, *Globalization – To What End?* (1992):

> it is worth recognizing that the recent splurge in globalization is part of an ongoing process with a long history. To begin with, capitalism was born in the process of creating a world market, and the long waves of growth in the core capitalist countries were associated with its centuries-long spread by conquest and economic penetration. In the past as in the present, competitive pressures, the incessant need for capital to keep on accumulating, and the advantages of controlling raw material sources have spurred business enterprise to reach beyond its

national borders .... While the expansion of capitalism has always presupposed and indeed required cooperation among its various national components ... there has never been a time when these same national components ceased to struggle each for its own preferment and advantage. Centrifugal and centripetal forces have always coexisted at the very core of the capitalist process, with sometimes one and sometimes the other predominating. As a result, periods of peace and harmony have alternated with periods of discord and violence. Generally, the mechanism of this alternation involves both economic and military forms of struggle, with the strongest power emerging victorious and enforcing acquiescence on the losers. But uneven development soon takes over, and a period of renewed struggle for hegemony emerges. (pp. 4–5)

The "strongest power" at present remains the United States, which has managed to maintain a global hegemonic imperialism since 1945. This hegemony has been under challenge from other leading capitalist countries since the 1970s. The United States has sought to maintain its preeminent position at every opportunity – through an expansion of its role as the leading military power, and by wielding its economic and financial might. "The fact that U.S. hegemonic imperialism proved to be so successful, and still continues to prevail," István Mészáros has explained in his *Socialism or Barbarism* (2001) – a work associated with the same broad tradition of Marxian analysis – "does not mean that it can be considered stable, let alone permanent. The envisaged 'global government' under U.S. management remains wishful thinking, like the 'Alliance for Democracy' and the 'Partnership for Peace,' projected – at a time of multiplying military collisions and social explosions – as the solid foundation of the newest version of the 'new world order.'" Instead what is emerging is the "potentially deadliest phase of imperialism" evident in: (1) growing rivalry between the United States, Europe and Japan; (2) increasing concern within U.S. ruling circles about the potential threat represented by China, viewed as an emerging superpower rival; and (3) aggressive U.S. attempts to preempt such challenges by extending the geopolitical sphere of its hegemony (*Socialism or Barbarism*, pp. 51–2). All the talk about globalization having integrated the world and disintegrated all centers, eliminating all sovereign powers, is largely illusion. Nation-state sovereignty and U.S. imperialism have not gone away but continue to exist in this new phase of capitalist globalization in an explosive mixture.

Globalization of capital in the present stage of capitalism is thus inseparable from increasing monopolization, that is, the concentration and centralization of capital on a world scale – which necessarily produces bigger contradictions and crises. "The three most important underlying trends in the recent history of capitalism, the period beginning with the recession of 1974–75," Sweezy argued in *Monthly Review* in 1997, were: "(1) the slowing down of the overall rate of growth, (2) the worldwide proliferation of monopolistic (or oligopolistic) multinational corporations, and (3) what may be called the financialization of the capital accumulation process." All of these underlying trends were a product of the driving force of capitalism, the capital accumulation process itself, rather than arising from globalization – which was to be seen as a process that has been going on as long as capitalism, but which could only be understood in terms of the latter. Nevertheless, all three of these "underlying trends," associated with capital accumulation, Sweezy was to emphasize, must be seen as taking place in "a context of continuing globalization which puts its imprint on the way the various processes play themselves out."[12]

What is perhaps most evident is that stagnation, monopolization, financialization, and the new phase of globalization, all combine to generate quite new and highly visible power mechanisms. As British political economist Michael Barratt Brown wrote in his *Models in Political Economy* (1995), "the system of production for profit in the market is still what organizes production. But the hand is no longer invisible, decisions are no longer unplanned. It is increasingly obvious that the hand is the hand of the managers of a few giant companies playing the market and planning the use of the world's resources to make money rather than to meet wants. More and more people can see this is so" (p. 37).

Rather than representing the realization of Adam Smith's invisible hand on a global scale – a seemingly inexorable mechanistic reality against which there is no recourse –

capitalism is more and more a contested sphere, in which concentration and centralization of production on a world scale and hence increasingly global competition between firms has its counterpart in the globalization of exploitation. Struggles over nation-state hegemony have not disappeared in this new stage of globalization, but continually resurface, often in more potent form.

Globalization as the end of history, as the end of nation-state sovereignty, as a new world order, as the integration of all peoples, or as a reality for which there is no alternative – are all myths carefully cultivated in our time. To see through these establishment myths – along with the "progressive" myth that we can oppose the instruments of neoliberal globalization without opposing the system itself – it is necessary to understand the historical changes associated with the development of monopoly capital on an increasingly global scale. Neither capitalism's monopolistic tendencies nor its imperialist divisions are in any way surmounted by the new globalization. At most these contradictions simply assume more universal forms. More than ever before a world of globalized monopoly capital and hegemonic imperialism, led by the United States, presents us with a stark choice: between a deadly barbarism or a humane socialism.

NOTES

1. The *New York Times* was encapsulating the views of Michael Hardt and Antonio Negri in their fashionable, postmodernist work, *Empire* (Cambridge, Mass.: Harvard University Press, 2000).
2. Much of the discussion in this and the following paragraphs draws on Paul M. Sweezy, "Monopoly Capitalism," in *New Palgrave Dictionary of Economics*, vol. 3 (New York: The Stockton Press, 1987), pp. 541–4.
3. All books by Steindl, Sweezy, Baran, Magdoff, Braverman and Mészáros mentioned in this essay are published by Monthly Review Press in New York.
4. Michal Kalecki, *Essays in the Theory of Economic Fluctuations* (London: Allen and Unwin, 1939), p. 149.
5. The monopoly capitalist economy does not consist simply of giant firms, of course. Within manufacturing, for example, there are hundreds of thousands of firms, which together employ a substantial share of the work force. These smaller firms are often attached to the giants, some supplying parts, others occupying various other niches. Such firms tend to bear the brunt of

an economic downturn. Conversely, during an expansion they tend to grow more rapidly than the dominant, monopolistic firms.

6. For a detailed discussion of Sweezy's views, from which part of this analysis is taken, see John Bellamy Foster, "Paul Marlor Sweezy," in Philip Arestis and Malcolm Sawyer, eds, *A Biographical Dictionary of Dissenting Economists* (Northampton, Mass.: Edward Elgar, 2000), pp. 642–51.

7. For a more thorough treatment of Baran's work, from which some of the present discussion is adapted, see John Bellamy Foster, "Paul Alexander Baran," in Arestis and Sawyer, eds, *A Biographical Dictionary of Dissenting Economists*, pp. 36–43.

8. Joanne Barkan, "A Blast from the Past: Paul A. Baran and Paul M. Sweezy's Monopoly Capital," *Dissent* 44, (Spring 1997), p. 95.

9. A fuller account of Braverman's ideas can be found in John Bellamy Foster, "Introduction," in Harry Braverman, *Labor and Monopoly Capital* (New York: Monthly Review Press, 1998), pp. ix–xxvii.

10. For a more extensive treatment of Magdoff's life and work, from which part of the present discussion has been drawn, see John Bellamy Foster, "Harry Magdoff," in Arestis and Sawyer, *A Biographical Dictionary of Dissenting Economists*, pp. 385–94.

11. A similar view, emanating from the third world, was presented in Samir Amin's pathbreaking work, *Accumulation on a World Scale* (New York: Monthly Review Press, 1974; first written as a dissertation in 1957).

12. Paul M. Sweezy, "More (or Less) on Globalization," *Monthly Review*, September 1997.

7   AMARTYA SEN:

The Late Twentieth Century's Greatest Political Economist?

Robin Hahnel

INTRODUCTION

It says much about the field of economics in the second half of the twentieth century that the man who might be the greatest political economist of his time would never consider himself to be a political economist at all. Amartya Sen would no doubt describe himself simply as a well-trained and well-read economist. He certainly would not identify as a "heterodox economist," i.e., an economist from one of the non-mainstream traditions. Nor should he. He is not a Marxist, Institutionalist or Post Keynesian economist, nor an ecological or feminist economist, much less a *radical* political economist – even though he studied for his doctorate at Cambridge University in the 1950s with the three greatest radical political economists of the day – Joan Robinson, Piero Sraffa, and Maurice Dobb. Yet Sen shares something in common with all those who self-identify with one heterodox school or another. The longer he studies the subject that most intrigues him, the more useless he finds mainstream economics to be.

A.K. Sen is a nit-picker. A.K. Sen is a contrarian. A.K. Sen suffers no fools. Since no school of economic thought has proven capable of answering the economic conundrum that most interests him to his satisfaction, Sen has stubbornly refused to swear allegiance to any tradition. In 1776 Adam Smith offered his answer to what he considered the principal economic question of his time: What is the cause of the wealth of nations? Sen is still searching for the answer to what he considers the principle economic question of our day: What is the cause of so much poverty in the midst of so much wealth and economic prosperity?

Sen has recently proposed a new theoretical framework for studying underdevelopment. For most of his 45 years as a professional economist he concentrated on demonstrating the inadequacies of mainstream approaches, and producing counter-intuitive gems of wisdom in the process. For most of his career he was content to lay bare anomalies in the "grand theories" of others, and displayed little inclination to offer alternatives of his own. After contributing to the axiomatic theory of social choice he concentrated on pointing out the fundamental inadequacies of neoclassical welfare theory. He assailed standard assumptions about famine and women in underdeveloped economies. He demolished standard measures of poverty and wellbeing. Only in the last few years has he moved from critic of others' theories to defender of a new theoretical framework of his own for studying underdevelopment and poverty. *Development as Freedom* (New York: Knopf and Oxford: Oxford University Press, 1999) was Sen's "coming out party" as a grand theorist. Predictably this has subjected him to unaccustomed criticisms from other nit-pickers who argue that his theory of entitlements and human capabilities holds less water than Sen claims, as well as objections from the powerful and privileged who are uncomfortable with the policy implications of his new approach.

Amartya Sen was awarded the Nobel Prize in economics in 1998 according to the Nobel jury for "several key contributions to the research on fundamental problems in welfare economics ranging from axiomatic theory of social choice to definitions of welfare and poverty indexes, to empirical studies of famine." For me the award not only provided long overdue recognition for Sen himself, but implicitly recognized the contributions of a whole generation of South Asian economists who are peerless in their knowledge of both mainstream and Marxist theory – while being advocates of neither. For me Amartya Sen is Dean of a school of South Asian economists who forswear all labels, celebrate methodological eclecticism, and are adept at applying whatever theoretical tools prove useful for shedding light on their defining interest: How do different economic institutions and policies affect the wretched of the earth? In his quest to make economics relevant to this question, Sen not only formulated subtle critiques of the philosophical underpinnings of traditional welfare economics and carried out ingenious empirical studies that demonstrate the transcendence of social over physical causes of famine and poverty himself, he also toiled in influential professional organizations and international agencies to give voice to important work by others on poverty and underdevelopment which otherwise would have gone ignored. In this essay I try to explain how his adept use of economic tools, his insights, his creativity, his patience, and his solidarity have combined to sharpen and focus many keen eyes on a truth that the economically powerful and their ideological servants within the mainstream of the economics profession constantly attempt to obfuscate: poverty is not self-inflicted. It is a social disease. However, I will also voice some criticisms and reservations about Sen's work, which at times I believe fails to be sufficiently "radical."

HIGH THEORY

From Capital Controversy to Social Choice Theory
Not surprisingly since Sen studied under Robinson, Sraffa and Dobb, his dissertation and earliest publications were concerned with theoretical issues prominent in the "capital controversy" raging between his professors in Cambridge England and the likes of Paul Samuelson and Robert Solow in Cambridge, Massachusetts. ("Choice of Capital-Intensity Further Considered," *Quarterly Journal of Economics 73*, 1959, *Choice of Techniques*, Oxford, Blackwell, 1960, "On Optimizing the Rate of Saving," *Economic Journal 71*, 1961, "Neoclassical and Neo-Keynesian Theories of Distribution," *Economic Record 39*, 1962, and "On the Usefulness of Used Machines," *Review of Economics and Statistics 44*, 1962.) Soon, however, Sen became intrigued by Kenneth Arrow's "Impossibility Theorem." He rejected the advice of his dissertation advisor, Joan Robinson (who thought the impossibility theorem was a waste of time and feared Sen would become enthralled in a worthless analytical

puzzle) and moved on to become a major figure in abstract social choice theory by the mid-1960s. ("Preferences, Votes and the Transitivity of Majority Decisions," *Review of Economic Studies 31*, 1964, "Mishan, Little and Welfare: A Reply," *Economic Journal 75*, 1965, "A Possibility Theorem on Majority Decisions," *Economica 34(2)*, 1966, "Quasi-Transitivity, Rational Choice and Collective Decision," *Review of Economic Studies 36(1)*, 1969, and *Collective Choice and Social Welfare*, Holden Day, 1970.) While this work "earned him his spurs" as one of the top theoretical economists in the world, Sen became increasingly critical of mainstream interpretations and applications of welfare economics, and turned his attention from refining the axiomatic theory of social choice toward pointing out the limitations of traditional welfare economics in general. In the end, contrary to the fear of his more radical mentor, Joan Robinson, Sen abandoned a field that turned out to be largely an analytical puzzle with few important implications – the capital controversy – to embrace a field – abstract social choice theory – that led Sen himself to reject the philosophical and methodological underpinnings of neoclassical welfare economics.

Sen's Critique of Welfare Theory
Sen began his critique of traditional welfare theory by picking apart inconsistencies in the theory of revealed preference that was highly popular in the profession at the end of the 1960s. ("Choice Functions and Revealed Preference," *Review of Economic Studies*, July 1971, "Behavior and the Concept of Preference," *Economica*, August 1973, "Choice, Orderings and Morality," in S. Korner, ed., *Practical Reason*, Oxford, Blackwell, 1974, and "Rational Fools," *Philosophy and Public Affairs*, Summer 1977.)[1] He began by pointing out that axioms of revealed preference theory such as consistency – if *a* is preferred to *b* then *b* cannot be preferred to *a* in some subsequent choice – and transitivity – if *a* is preferred to *b* and *b* is preferred to *c* then *a* must be preferred to *c* – are not likely to hold when people's tastes, or "choice functions" change over time. For this reason Sen predicted that empirical support for revealed preference theory as a theory of actual human behavior would always prove disappointing. He went on to explain that it was not only

predictable, but indeed fortuitous that people often did not behave in accord with the dictates of individual rationality as assumed by revealed preference theory. Sen explained this point in his typically felicitous way:

> I have no competence whatever to throw light on the psychological issues underlying these problems. Instead I shall try to discuss one and a half other issues which seem to me to be also important. The half issue should perhaps come first ... . Suppose it is the case that there are strong environmental reasons for using glass bottles for distributing soft drinks (rather than single-use steel cans) and for persuading the customers to return the bottles to the shops from where they buy these drinks (rather than disposing of them in the dustbin). For a relatively rich country the financial incentives offered for returning the bottles may not be adequate if the consumers neither worry about the environment nor are thrilled by receiving back small change. The environment affects the life of all, true enough, but from the point of view of any one individual the harm that he can do to the environment by adding his bottles to those of others will be exceedingly tiny. Being generally interested in the environment but also being lazy about returning bottles, this person may be best off if the others return bottles but not he, next best if all return bottles, next best if none does, and worst of all if he alone returns bottles while others do not. If others feel in a symmetrical way we shall then be in a prisoners' dilemma type situation in which people will not return bottles but at the same time all would have preferred that all of them should return bottles rather than none. To tackle this problem, suppose now that people are persuaded that non-return is a highly irresponsible behaviour, and while the individuals in question continue to have exactly the same view of their welfare, they fall prey to ethical persuasion, political propaganda, or moral rhetoric. The welfare functions and the preference relations are still exactly the same and all that changes is behaviour. The result is good for the environment but sad for the theory of revealed preference ... . It is not necessary that people have concern for others, but if they behave *as if* they have this concern, they will end up being better off in terms of their real preference. This is where the revealed preference approach goes off the rails altogether. The behaviour pattern that will make each better off in

terms of their real preferences is not at all the behaviour pattern that will *reveal* those real preferences ... . I would argue that the philosophy of the revealed preference approach essentially underestimates the fact that man is a social animal. ("Behavior and the Concept of Preference," *Economica*, August 1973)

By 1976 Sen had moved on from carefully criticizing to ridiculing the behavioral foundations of economic theory. In his celebrated lecture honoring Herbert Spencer at Oxford University titled "Rational Fools" Sen refuted the assumption that people always behave out of self-interest by illustrating its absurdity in a simple example revealing how nonsensical life would be if people really did behave purely out of self-interest:

> "Where is the railway station?" He asks me. "There," I say, pointing at the post office, "and would you please post this letter for me on the way?" "Yes," he says, determined to open the envelope and check whether it contains something valuable.

He went on in the same lecture to distinguish between sympathy, and commitment – and argued that, ironically, behavior based on commitment was more problematic than behavior based on sympathy for a purely egotistical theory of human behavior.

> If the knowledge of torture of others makes you sick, it is a case of sympathy. If it does not make you feel personally worse off, but you think it is wrong and you are ready to do something to stop it, it is a case of commitment.

Sen's point was that in the case of sympathy a donation to Amnesty International could be interpreted as self-interested, or egotistical, but in the case of commitment it cannot because the donor has chosen an alternative they believe will yield a lower level of personal welfare for them than an alternative that is also available to them – namely not to donate but instead to "ride for free" on the donations of others.

The instant popularity of "Rational Fools" was testament to the fact that Sen had hit on a raw nerve for many who feel that they, and their fellow "good citizens," often behave out of commitment to their personal detriment, and who resent economic theory for assuming otherwise. Worse still, when economic theory teaches it is "good citizens" who are fools for failing to individually maximize and free ride on the "committed" behavior of others, it rubs more salt in the wound. Little wonder so many reacted with glee when Sen turned the tables on their neoclassical accusers, labeling them the "rational fools."

In "Choice Orderings and Morality" (*Practical Reason*, S. Korner, ed., Oxford, 1974) Sen moved on from observing that, contrary to the assumptions of revealed preference theory, people *do* engage in non-egotistical "committed" behavior, and no society would be viable if they did not, to arguing that social norms and customs could be seen as vehicles to avoid inefficient outcomes in social choice situations by substituting committed behavior for egotistical behavior. Sen compared the outcome of a Prisoners' Dilemma (PD) game – where only an enforceable contract avoids inferior outcomes for all – to the outcome of an Assurance Game (AG) – where a simple commitment that would *not* require policing avoids inferior outcomes for all – to the outcome of an Other-Regarding Game (OR) – where optimal outcomes occur automatically. He pointed out that, not only would people obviously all fare better if people all actually had the kind of preferences that gave rise to OR and AG games rather than PD games in situations of social choice, but that *even if* people actually had PD (selfish) preferences, they would all be better off if they behaved *as if* they had OR (sympathetic) or AG (committed) preferences. From this Sen concluded: "It is tempting to rank the three pairs of preferences in a moral order: OR preferences, AG preferences, and PD preferences, and society may evolve traditions by which preferences of the OR-type are praised most, AG-type preferences next, and PD-preferences least of all." Sen pointed to norms and customs as precisely the means whereby society praised or rewarded socially productive OR and AG preferences and criticized or penalized socially counterproductive PD preferences.

Sen's most important break with mainstream welfare theory came, however, when he realized that the ban on interpersonal utility comparisons made it an insurmountable obstacle to approaching issues of social choice "rationally." Many before him had come to this conclusion more directly by asking: if we are unwilling to compare benefits that accrue to some at the expense of costs to others, how can we possibly expect to have much to say about the desirability of many, if not most social choices? By contrast, Sen came to this conclusion the hard way, and perhaps for that reason became all the more adamant, insisting that rational discussion of social choice *must* successfully prioritize *different kinds of consequences* to *different kinds of people.*

Sen's hard road began by exploring conceivable ways out of Arrow's theorem which showed the impossibility of aggregating individual preferences into a rule of social choice satisfying four conditions – all of which appear quite reasonable. (1) Unrestricted Domain, U: the rule must apply to every logically possible combination of individual preferences. (2) The weak Pareto principle, P: if everyone prefers one outcome over another then the social choice rule must rank the outcome everyone prefers over the other. (3) Non-dictatorship, D: there is no one person such that whenever they prefer any outcome over any other outcome, then the social choice rule invariably ranks that outcome over the other. (4) Independence of irrelevant alternatives, I: the social ranking of any two outcomes must remain the same as long as the individual utility information about the pair of outcomes remains the same, which, in the case of ordinal, non-comparable utilities, amounts to individual orderings over the pair remaining the same. Sen took Arrow's impossibility theorem to heart. If it was merely a technical "trick," then it could be reasonably circumvented and rational debate over social choice could proceed, using mainstream theory. If, however, it was substantively, as well as technically true, Sen recognized that economists would be much more limited in what they could say about social choice than Sen wanted to believe. So he had to figure out what made Arrow's theorem "tick."

Characteristically, he began by strengthening the theorem to eliminate questioning assumptions that would not get him out of his dilemma in any case. In this vein, for example, Sen showed that the theorem – and therefore the dilemma for social choice theory – held even if individual preferences were assumed to be cardinal instead of ordinal. Together with Prasant Pattanaik, he then proceeded to strengthen work by Arrow, Black, Inada, Vickrey and Ward who had proposed weakening the assumption of unlimited domain by restricting individual preference combinations to be what they called "single-peaked" to allow majority rule to satisfy Arrow's remaining conditions for a reasonable social welfare rule – P, D, and I. Essentially, if individuals classify alternatives in terms of a single dimension – like how politically "left," "right," or "centrist" the alternative is – and in any pair-wise choice vote for the alternative which is closer to their own position, then individual preference patterns will be "single-peaked" and majority decision will be transitive, i.e., there will be some alternative that enjoys a majority over every other possible alternative. Nonetheless, even after weakening restrictions others had placed on the domain set of combinations of individual preferences in order for majority rule to satisfy the remaining conditions, Sen was forced to conclude:

> It is clear that these results can be interpreted as being "comforting" typically only in those choice situations in which the set of alternatives is rather limited, e.g., choosing between a few candidates in an election, or deciding in an assembly between some alternative proposals. In the economic problems of allocation and distribution involving a rich commodity space, there is little chance that the required conditions [single peaked preferences] will be fulfilled. Indeed, it is easily checked that even for the elementary problem of the distribution of a given cake between three or more persons with each preferring more cake for himself, the majority preference relation will be intransitive .... To illustrate, with any given division of the cake, take away half the share of the worst-off person and divide the loot among the rest. We have just made a majority "improvement." If we are ambitious and want *more* social improvement, we repeat the exercise! The majority rule cannot really serve as the basis of welfare economic judgments dealing with interest conflicts, and this can be seen even without considering the question of consistency at all. (*Choice, Welfare and Measurement,* Harvard University Press, 1982 pp. 12–13)

It was a short step from realizing that no restrictions on individual preferences that left people caring about their own share at all could make the majority decision rule a reasonable social choice rule where distributing benefits was involved, to the conclusion that the "secret" that "dooms Arrow's aggregation exercise to failure was the imposed poverty of the utility information" (*Choice, Welfare and Measurement*, p. 18), by which Sen meant the ban on interpersonal comparisons of utility. When Sen reconsidered the cake division problem under Arrow's assumption of interpersonal incomparability he discovered a startling result.

> Consider again the cake division problem and take two different cases. In case A, person 1 is very rich while 2 and 3 are poor, whereas in case B, person 1 is very poor while 2 and 3 are rich. In both cases we consider a redistribution – cutting out a bit from person 1's share of the cake and dividing that gain between 2 and 3. If each person prefers more cake to himself (i.e., if we make the standard assumption for the cake division exercise) then persons 2 and 3 prefer the change while person 1 disprefers it, in both cases A and B. Now the question: are the two cases of redistribution exactly similar? In the Arrow format they have to be. Suppose we want to say that the redistribution is more justified in case A than in case B, how would we distinguish the two cases? It is tempting to point out that person 1 is *worse off* than the others in case B but not so in case A. But if by "worse off" we mean having lower utility, then that type of statement is ruled out by the absence of interpersonal comparisons of utility. If, on the other hand, by worse off we mean having less cake and thus being poorer, that type of non-utility information cannot be taken into account due to exclusive reliance on utility information only. Indeed, in the Arrow format the two cases are *informationally identical,* and exactly the same judgment must be made about the change in both the cases, since the individual preference orderings are identical in the two cases … . Arrow's remarkable achievement was to show – though he did not put it this way – that in such an informational format there are no consistent non-dictatorial rules. It does not belittle the outstanding importance of this elegant and far-reaching logical result to note that an informational format that cannot distinguish between cases A and B

is quite unsuitable *anyway* for welfare economics. More information is needed to deal with interest conflicts. The unsuitable, it transpires, is also impossible. (*Choice, Welfare and Measurement*: pp. 19–20)

Sen's pilgrimage through late-twentieth-century high theory led him squarely to reject its most salient assumption, namely that social choice theory should be approached without presuming to make interpersonal utility comparisons. He had convinced himself not only that social choice theory *should not* proceed under this severe informational restriction, but that it *could not* proceed under such a restriction. Sen had not only successfully escaped Arrow's impossibility theorem, he had re-interpreted the theorem as "proof" that without interpersonal comparability there are no consistent non-dictatorial rules in economic situations where a theory of social choice is required in the first place! In his own words:

Not only is the Arrow impossibility theorem a remarkable result, of great analytical beauty, it is also surprisingly robust, *given* the informational constraints. Recent works in weakening the conditions of social transitivity, binariness of social choice, independence conditions and unrestricted domain, have revealed how easy it is to get trapped in an Arrow-like impossibility result as one escapes the exact impossibility pinpointed in Arrow's theorem. On the other hand, genuine escape routes emerge with real possibility results once the informational constraints are lifted or weakened. ("Personal Utilities and Public Judgments: or What's Wrong with Welfare Economics?" *Economic Journal 89*, September 1979)

Convinced that adding information was the right road to follow, Sen proceeded to overcome the Arrovian poverty of information he had discovered to be the chief obstacle to progress in mainstream social choice theory. First he explored different ways to make interpersonal comparisons of utility. Next he considered ways to incorporate important non-utility information. In "On Weights and Measures: Informational Constraints in Social Welfare Analysis" (*Economica 45*, October 1977) he showed how different kinds of interpersonal comparability permitted well-known social choice rules like utilitarianism and the "difference principle" of John Rawls to satisfy Arrow's conditions. In "Ignorance and Equal Distribution" (*American Economic Review 63*, December 1973), "Interpersonal Aggregation and Partial Comparability" (*Economica 38*, May 1978), and "On Interpersonal Comparisons of Welfare" (*Economics and Human Welfare: Essays in Honor of Tibor Scitovsky*, M. Beskin, ed., Academic Press, 1979) Sen explored his hypothesis that "interpersonal utility comparisons may be neither impossible nor – on the other hand – terribly exact." In a series of articles he tried to give more rigorous expression to what he sensed was "a common attitude towards interpersonal comparisons of utility which involves neither Pigouvian precision nor Robbinsian rejection" (*Choice, Welfare and Measurement*, pp. 22–3). In "Interpersonal Aggregation and Partial Comparability" (*Econometrica 38*, May 1970), he worked hard to lay "the formal basis for judgments that are not consistent with non-comparability but which do not require full comparability, and to develop a continuum of intermediate assumptions."

Sen began adding non-utility conditions to make a social choice rule more acceptable by trying to correct for a common objection to majority rule – that it is *illiberal* in the sense that there are some decisions where an individual's preferences should be "sovereign," i.e., should not be subject to overrule by others. However, when he added a libertarian condition he discovered a surprising new impossibility theorem: "A principle reflecting liberal values (later re-named libertarian values) even in a very mild form cannot possibly be combined with the weak Pareto principle given an unrestricted domain." "The Impossibility of a Paretian Liberal" (*Journal of Political Economy 78*, January 1970) unleashed a flurry of attempts to escape the conflict between the two principles since the Paretian principle was commonly considered an *expression*, not violator of individual liberty. Sen himself argued that the implications of his impossibility theorem were not as discouraging as many seemed to think. He tried to soften the blow by pointing out that "the conflict arises with only particular configurations of individual preferences" permitted by the condition of unrestricted domain, and by observing that "the ultimate guarantee for individual liberty may not rest on rules for social choice but on developing individual values that respect each other's personal choices" ("Liberty, Unanimity and Rights," *Economica 43*, August 1976). Nonetheless, he persisted that utilitarianism, even in the weak Paretian form, was at odds with libertarian values to a greater extent than many economists had previously recognized.

Critique of Sen's Critique
I admire Sen's technical virtuosity, endorse his rejection of revealed preference theory as a methodologically confused and fundamentally flawed theory of actual human behavior, and agree with his conclusion that social choice theory is impossible without interpersonal comparability, and morally unacceptable without some kinds of non-utility considerations. On the other hand, I marvel at important points he missed in his critique of mainstream welfare theory and question the usefulness of where Sen would lead us in the domain of "high theory."

Most mainstream theorists persist in presenting analyses of individual rationality as a theory to *explain* and *predict* actual human behavior. In a famous article George Stigler and Gary Becker even extended the mainstream theory to, in their words, "four classes of phenomenon widely believed to be inconsistent with the stability of tastes: addiction, habitual behavior, advertising, and fashions, and in each case offered an alternative explanation consistent with individual rational choice" ("De Gustibus Non Est Disputandum," *American Economic Review*, March 1977). So it is understandable that Sen would rail with all his might against the absurdity of interpreting human behavior in this way, but in his haste to reject individual rationality as a compelling theory of actual human behavior, Sen failed to appreciate the true usefulness of a theory of individual rationality. If we wish to know what impact an economic institution has on human behavior, we must evaluate the kind of behavior that institution promotes. If we ask how institutions "promote" one kind of behavior rather than another, the answer is they do so by making some behavior individually rational and other behavior individually irrational, and that is where a theory of individual rational choice logically enters the stage: we need to know what it would be rational for an individual to do given their own priorities, or preferences, when making choices in a particular institutional context. In other words, the subject of choice theoretic welfare theory should not be to predict actual human behavior, but instead to evaluate the effects of particular economic institutions on human behavior. *Welfare theory is not a theory for predicting human behavior but a theory for evaluating economic institutions.*[2] Unfortunately Sen is joined by a majority of progressive and heterodox economists who also fail to understand how the theory of rational choice can provide a powerful critique of economic institutions by demonstrating how they create incentives for people to behave in individually rational but socially counterproductive ways.[3] Instead, like Sen, when progressives correctly reject rational choice theory as a compelling theory of actual human behavior, they also throw the baby out with the bath water and never consider its usefulness as a means to criticize economic institutions.

It is also surprising that Sen has little to contribute to a theory of preference development. He observed early on that consistency and transitivity were unlikely when people's preferences change, and he was thoroughly conversant with the work of others who explored theories of endogenous preference. Moreover, Sen displayed a keen interest in what kind of preferences people had for both technical and substantive reasons. Weakening the assumption of unrestricted domain – requiring "single peaked preferences", for example – affords ways out of Arrow's impossibility dilemma. Other directed and committed preferences often generate socially efficient outcomes, whereas selfish preferences do not, and hopes of reconciling libertarianism with Paretian efficiency lie in people having tolerant preferences. Sen discovered all this, yet failed to explore *why* people might "rationally" develop some kinds of preferences rather than others.[4] Again, he failed to see that particular economic institutions like markets, private enterprise, or central planning for that matter, make it individually rational to develop some kinds of preferences and not others, including the kinds of preferences Sen lamented.[5] Sen limited his observations about preference development to providing a new rationale for why some preferences could be described as "more moral" than others, and pointing out that cultural norms could be interpreted as supporting "more moral" preferences. However, in this I fear Sen contributed little beyond what was already common knowledge among mainstream sociologists. In sum, by failing to see the theory of individual rational choice as a powerful tool for critically evaluating the effect of economic institutions on people's behavior and their patterns of preference development, but instead rejecting the theory *in toto* because it is a poor theory of actual human behavior, Sen missed a major opportunity to advance the cause of a critical evaluation of the major economic institutions of our day. Instead he improved upon mainstream economists' theory of human behavior by recognizing the logic of committed behavior, but still lagged behind mainstream psychology and sociology in a field – predicting actual human behavior – that simply is not economists' comparative advantage!

I also doubt Sen's painstaking technical work developing different degrees of partial interpersonal utility comparability will prove the basis for further progress in social choice theory for the simple reason that interpersonal comparability is fundamentally a philosophical, not a technical issue. Sen's inclination was to approach comparability as a technical exercise in metrics rather than a philosophical issue of distributive justice – which I believe it must inevitably be. The question – "What is an equitable distribution of burdens and benefits of socially organized economic activity?" – will not go away no matter how long economists continue to avoid addressing it head-on because it is controversial.

Finally, I am not inclined to follow Sen's lead when he does delve into philosophy. The impossibility of a Paretian liberal, like Arrow's impossibility theorem, was an ingenious theorem, but it is simply a clever way of making the same point many philosophers have made before, regarding the fundamental difference – and incompatibility – of utilitarian and social contract theories of justice.[6] Moreover, by limiting his philosophical explorations to utilitarianism and libertarianism, I fear Sen has fallen victim to inherent weakness in two theories that have dominated liberal debates over social justice for the past three centuries and have little left to teach us. Instead I believe it will prove to be the case that progressives are better served by using different concepts to treat economic efficiency, democracy, and justice, and to establish explicit priorities if and when these different economic goals prove to be in conflict. In my view the Pareto principle – with a proper theory of endogenous preferences – is an adequate theory of economic efficiency. Self-management, defined as decision-making input in proportion to the degree one is affected, is the legitimate way to apportion economic decision-making power among people. Economic reward based on personal sacrifice, or effort, (rather than contribution), tempered by consideration for special needs, is the best approximation to economic justice.[7] By continuing the search for a non-controversial, over-arching theory of social choice that attempts to incorporate economic efficiency, equity and democracy, Sen leads us away from where I believe we must go, no matter how much he contributed to undermining the vacuous theory of social choice to which the mainstream of our profession clings to this day.

BRUTAL REALITY

Famine: Not Simply for Lack of Food
As a nine-year-old Sen witnessed the Bengal famine of 1943 that killed 2 to 3 million people. In the 1970s and 1980s, together with Jean Dreze, Sen undertook an extensive empirical study of famines (*Hunger and Public Action*, 1989, and *The Political Economy of Hunger*, 3 volumes, 1990–91, Oxford, Clarendon Press) which demonstrated that distributional failures resulting from faulty economic and political institutions were more frequent causes of famine than insufficient food production resulting from natural disasters. Dreze and Sen discovered that in the Bengal famine of 1943 people died in front of well-stocked food shops protected by the state. They discovered that in Bangladesh in 1974 there was *greater* food availability per person than in any year between 1971 and 1976 but, because they had no land of their own, rural laborers' incomes came from transplanting rice for others, and the floods kept them from earning the meager

amount necessary to keep themselves and their families alive. They discovered that in Ireland in the 1840s and in Ethiopia in 1973 food moved *out* of famine areas because income, and therefore "effective demand," was lower there than in areas where people were not starving. They discovered also that since 1950, while China, in general, has done a better job than India in eliminating hunger, there have been no famines in India whereas millions died in famines in China between 1958 and 1961. This anomaly led Sen and Dreze to emphasize the importance of an independent media and democratic government in preventing famine. An independent media makes it difficult to suppress embarrassing news, and democracy makes governments at least vulnerable to embarrassment.

Missing Females
After challenging the way many international agencies approach famine prevention and relief, Sen turned his attention to gender issues in economic development, arguing that low levels of development affect women more adversely than men. In 1990 he published an article in the *New York Review of Books* titled "More than 100 Million Women Are Missing," where he popularized findings he published in scientific journals ("Women's Survival as a Development Problem," *Bulletin of the American Academy of Arts and Sciences*, 1989, and "Missing Women," *British Medical Journal*, 1992). Sen translated the effects of parental preference for sons and unequal access to food and healthcare for husbands and wives in poor families in developing countries into terms difficult to ignore, calculating that if women were treated by their families in the same way that men are treated, there would be at least another 100 million women alive today! Sen further demonstrated a clear correlation between missing females and patriarchal power, showing that there were fewer missing females in countries where women were more independent and had more control over resources like land. Again, Sen's work changed policy in some international development projects leading them to provide food directly to children rather than to patriarchal households, and prioritizing employment of mothers outside the household, which Sen showed vastly improved well-being for mothers *and* children alike.

SYNTHESIS: MEASURING FAILURE AND SUCCESS

Beginning in the 1980s Sen began to combine his work in social choice theory with his practical investigations of hunger, famine and the mortal effects of patriarchy by refining standard measures of poverty and economic development.

Poverty Indices

Traditionally economists have measured poverty by finding the level of income necessary to sustain families of different sizes and types and then calculating the percentage of families that fall below this poverty line. Sen pointed out a number of flaws in this approach. (1) It only considers income, so a person of moderate means but very high medical expenses would not be classified as poor even though their income after paying for medical expenses might be negligible. (2) There is conflict as well as cooperation in families, so while a family might have sufficient income to place it above the poverty line, women and children might live in poverty within the family if the patriarch is not benevolent. (3) As poverty rates are traditionally calculated, if the government took money from a poor family far below the poverty line and gave it to another family just under the poverty line, moving the second family above the poverty line, the measured rate of poverty would fall even though "poverty" would obviously increase. The Sen poverty index ("Poverty: An Ordinal Approach to Measurement," *Econometrica 44(2)*, 1976) at least remedied the last problem by giving greater weight to those farther below the poverty line. Sen proposed analogous modifications of the Gini coefficient, the usual measure of overall inequality of income or wealth, giving greater weight to those at the bottom of the distribution so that a reduction of inequality at the top of the distribution would not entirely cancel an equal increase of inequality at the bottom of the distribution.

Human Development Indices

Moving beyond measuring economic success in terms of income alone required developing a more elaborate index of economic wellbeing than income per capita, and selling the idea to important international organizations. Sen worked for years as a consultant to the UN, helping construct a summary index that would capture the extent to which basic opportunities were available to people. The Human Development Index (HDI) first appeared in the United Nation's *Human Development Report*, an alternative to the World Bank's *World Development Report*, in 1990. The HDI is a weighted average of income per capita adjusted for purchasing power, income inequality, life expectancy, literacy, and average years of education. How one measures economic success can make a great difference. Sri Lanka, Vietnam and Cuba rank much higher among all countries on the HDI index than they do according to income per capita, and Canada, whose per capita income ranks it below many other developed countries, had the highest HDI index in the world a few years ago due to low income inequality and high literacy and longevity.

GRAND THEORY

Capabilities and Entitlements

Sen began his search for an alternative to mainstream welfare theory by embracing the "basic needs perspective" pioneered by development economist Paul Streeten in the late 1970s and early 1980s. This approach focused attention on the unacceptable kinds of lives people are forced to live when their fundamental needs are not met, and insisted that *everyone* have access to the goods and services necessary for meeting their *basic needs* before less pressing desires of the better-off are addressed. Sen expanded the basic needs approach by distinguishing between production and exchange *entitlements*, pointing out that small farmers and share croppers have production entitlements whereas laborers have exchange entitlements. This distinction can be important, because during normal times the exchange entitlements of a laborer usually allow him to command more commodities than a small farmer or sharecropper, but in the event of a natural disaster, the production entitlements of farmers and sharecroppers are more likely to be effective in helping them meet their basic needs. Sen also explained how cultural, kinship and political institutions can augment or reduce entitlements.

By focusing on different types of entitlements Sen broadened concerns beyond the traditional concern of economists – how to maximize output. He soon realized, however, that the basic needs approach was subject to criticisms similar to those he had raised against traditional welfare economics: how does one distinguish between needs that are basic and those that are not? Are basic needs biologically determined or time- and place-dependent? What can be said about changes in the degree of inequality among those whose basic needs are met? Or, for that matter, among those whose basic needs are not met? If we favor greater equality, equality of what? In attempting to answer these questions, Sen began to focus more on what people can do and less on the goods they receive. He argued that the kind of equality we should promote is equality of opportunity, and he moved from the satisfaction of basic needs to expanding people's *capabilities*. According to the capability approach literacy is important, not because of the utility it yields, but because it expands people's capability to acquire information. Voting is important, not because of any intrinsic satisfaction derived from it, but because it expands people's capability to express their will over social decisions. Clothes are important both because they protect people from the cold or heat – basic needs – *and* for reasons of self-respect and social respect. For this reason it may require more expensive clothes for someone living in Beverly Hills to have the "capability of being respected" than for someone in Bangladesh. So, while the capability, respect, is absolute, the goods required to achieve it may be relative. In any case, for Sen: (1) the real goal of economic development is to increase people's capabilities; (2) we should be wary that any proxy measure of progress toward that goal is likely to prove misleading in some circumstances; (3) increasing the capabilities of the less capable should take precedence over improving the capabilities of those who are already more capable.

Development as Freedom
In *Development as Freedom* Sen goes beyond the capabilities approach and argues that development can be defined as the

expansion of freedom, i.e., that all the capabilities people may acquire are to be understood as exemplifying freedom. In his desire to describe all the "good" things that come with "development" as expansions of "freedom" Sen talks, for example, about mortality as a denial of "the freedom to survive." Paul Seabright took exception to reducing development to the expansion of freedoms in the March 29, 2001 issue of *The New York Review of Books*. "Well yes, one can call death denial of the freedom to survive. But is it really illuminating to suggest that what matters about being dead is the lack of freedom that goes with it? Being dead is also bad for the health and has a significant statistical association with dropping out of college, but personally I think it's the deadness that would bother me ... . We can always *say* that the society we like best is the one that most advances freedom, but a claim of that kind sounds remarkably like the claim in Molière that opium sends people to sleep because of its dormitive faculty."

CONCLUSION

I have already explained where I think Sen's critique of mainstream welfare theory both hits, and misses, the mark. I should add that I find Sen far more intellectually persuasive in the role of critic than creator. He provides a devastating critique of the economic establishment's pretense to a theory of social choice without admitting interpersonal comparisons of wellbeing or non-utility considerations. His criticisms of standard procedures for measuring economic progress and poverty are irrefutable and compelling. In criticism he is meticulous and his technical virtuosity is everywhere apparent. However, it is when he turns to the task of developing alternatives to the theories and measures he criticizes so successfully that I believe his work becomes intellectually less compelling. As I mentioned earlier, for such a great student of the theory of rational choice and preferences to have missed the opportunity to put rational choice theory to good use as a tool for criticizing economic institutions and for explaining why people "rationally" develop socially counterproductive preferences, is both mysterious and unfortunate. Likewise, while I applaud emphasizing basic-need fulfillment over growth in average income, and what people can *do*, rather than what they have, I do not think Sen provides an entirely successful intellectual defense for these approaches to poverty and development against many traditional objections. On the other hand, for the past thirty years there has been no more effective spokesperson than Amartya Sen for those who object to judging human progress by the rate of growth of marketed output.

Judging human progress by the rate of growth of the market value of goods and services per capita is both ignorant and malevolent, and all who speak out against this common practice are more than justified. It is ignorant because economic progress is only one component of human progress. Life expectancy, health, literacy, education, political and civil rights, and a host of other concerns are all relevant to whether or not humans are "progressing." It is ignorant because what truly matters is what economic wherewithal permits people to *do*, not the wherewithal itself. It is ignorant because growth in the market value of gross output is not the same as growth in the social value of gross output. Market prices often diverge considerably from true social values, and a great deal of socially valuable production is never recorded in a market transaction. It is ignorant because growth in the social value of gross output is not the same as growth in the social value of net output. Deterioration, not only of produced capital, but natural capital as well, and production of "bads" like pollution that accompanies production of "goods," obviously need to be taken into account when calculating economic progress. It is ignorant because the distribution of economic progress among people matters a great deal. Economic progress hinges as much on improvements in economic justice as in economic efficiency. It is ignorant because no matter how efficient or just economic outcomes may be, the *way* in which economic decisions are made matters as well. Economic progress hinges on improvements in economic democracy just as it does on improvements in economic justice and efficiency. Measuring human progress by the rate of growth of the market value of goods and services per capita is malevolent because it serves the personal agendas of powerful economic, political, cultural and kinship elites at the expense of the interests of people at large. Lack of progress in non-economic areas, lack of progress in economic justice and democracy, and increasing environmental degradation all go unnoticed when human development is equated with mis-measured economic growth. Sen has thrown the full weight of his intellectual stature and standing in professional organizations of economists behind pointing out all these mistakes whenever and wherever they are practiced.

There are two possible responses to this ignorant and malevolent practice: (1) design a more comprehensive and inclusive indicator of human progress, or (2) insist that economic progress should not be equated with human progress, and that economic progress should not be equated with the rate of growth of marketed output, but instead, that human *and* economic progress be measured along a number of different dimensions. The two approaches have a great deal in common. Both must point out the ignorance and malevolence of the standard practice of conflation. Both must develop ways to measure all the important components of human progress other than growth of marketed output. In both cases legitimate debate concerns (a) whether or not to include a particular dimension, and (b) how best to define and measure progress along any particular dimension. However, for those, like Sen, who attempt to design a comprehensive indicator of human progress, debate over appropriate weights for the different dimensions in the index is inevitable as well. In the second approach, avoiding debate over appropriate weights is bought at the expense of multiple, conflicting judgments about how well human beings are progressing. I am inclined toward the latter approach because I cannot imagine how a debate over weights will increase our understanding of how much, or little, we are "progressing," and because I suspect futile debate over weights will replace more productive discussions about what are the important dimensions of human progress and how best to measure them. I also fear that a single index could serve political regimes as an excuse to justify deficiencies in some areas by overall gains according to the index *even though the advance in the overall index might have been possible to achieve without losses along neglected dimensions.* However, my quarrel with Sen, and with others who have constructed overall indicators, is not so much over whether or not to do so, but what dimensions to include in an overall indicator of human progress and how to define them.

Sen and his collaborators at the UN included measures of health, education, and income distribution along with economic growth in their Human Development Index, or HDI, but they ignored concerns with democracy and the environment. Others working at Redefining Progress have come up with an index they call the Genuine Progress Indicator, or GPI, that incorporates environmental degradation along with income distribution and economic growth. But they ignore education, health and democracy. In both cases the index is misleading as an indicator of human progress because of omitted dimensions. Other indices such as the gender disparity index, GDI, the gender empowerment measure, GEM, and the Heritage Foundation economic freedom index, all focus on measuring a single dimension of progress other than economic growth. In the case of single dimension indices such as these the question is whether or not the definition of the goal and/or the method of measurement is appropriate. In some cases the definition is appropriate and method of measurement judicious. But in other cases the index is highly suspect. For example, in my view the Heritage Foundation's economic freedom index is an ideological subterfuge that does little to advance the cause of measuring the extent to which people control their economic destinies in different national economies. The general problem with single dimension indices is, however, that even if they define and measure one goal well, it is only one dimension of human progress. On the other hand, the problem with indices that claim to be comprehensive is that, even if particular dimensions are defined and measured appropriately, omitted dimensions render them useless, and challenging the weights used is always a logical rebuttal. In any case, I have yet to see any index purporting to be an indicator of overall human progress that is not seriously flawed by obviously omitted variables.

I also find much in Sen's theory of capacities, entitlements, and economic development as the expansion of freedom problematic. If the study of poverty is to be different from the study of economic justice and injustice, and if measuring poverty is to be different from measuring inequality of income and wealth, then there must be a line to divide the poor from the not-poor, and some way to defend where that line is drawn. Also, if there is a meaningful line, then moving someone across that line must be more meaningful than moving someone an equal distance, but not across the line. I have no objection to placing greater weight on improving the economic situation of anyone who is worse off than effecting an equal improvement for someone who is better off, as Sen proposes, but that constitutes neither a justification for doing so, nor an answer to the question of whether, and how, we should draw a poverty line. If it is difficult to decide what needs are basic and what needs are not, then it is just as difficult to decide what capacities, and entitlements to those capacities, should be prioritized and which should not. In other words, I think Sen has not solved some long-standing conceptual problems in the field of economic development. Nonetheless, Sen deserves more credit than any other single individual for moving international organizations like the United Nations, and to some extent regional development banks and the World Bank, toward a more comprehensive and meaningful view of economic development and its measurement.

Finally, I agree with Paul Seabright that redefining everything that it is good for someone to have as an increase in their freedom to have it may be good salesmanship in the era of the free market jubilee, but it is not good methodology. First of all, by conflating all "goods" into one – freedom – we not only reduce the power of language, we risk deceiving ourselves that something is more simple than it really is – a mistake Sen warned others against for most of his intellectual life. Economic development is *not* simply the expansion of freedoms. Second, all too often when one person's freedom expands it does so at the expense of someone else's freedom that contracts. It is no less ambiguous and problematic when Amartya Sen says the goal of economic development is to maximize people's freedom than when Milton Friedman said the most important economic goal was to maximize economic freedom (*Capitalism as Free-*

dom, University of Chicago Press, 1964). What are we to do when people's freedoms conflict? When forced to choose between polluters' freedom to pollute and pollution victims' freedom to be pollution-free? Between employers' freedom to use their capital as they see fit and employees' freedom to use their laboring capacities as they would like? Friedman is happy to leave the answer to these problems of conflicting personal freedoms to the reigning property rights system. Presumably Sen is not, but if not, then how are we to prioritize some freedoms over others and the freedoms of some people over the freedoms of other people? That is why I prefer the concept of self-management – defined as decision-making power in proportion to the degree one is affected – to the concept of economic freedom – defined as the freedom to do whatever one wants with one's person and property. Finally, by embracing the metaphor of economic freedom Sen encourages the dominant rationalization for exploitation of our times. If people freely choose to enter into an arrangement, how can the outcome be considered unjust? This is the common response to legitimate complaints that wages are exploitative, that giant corporations price gouge, that the international credit system is usurious, and that free trade is unequal exchange. I am not suggesting that Sen himself falls victim to this sophistry, but the freedom-encompasses-all metaphor he proposes easily lends itself to abuse, particularly if those who know better, such as Sen, are not forthright in denouncing the machinations of the merchants of global capital.

For similar reasons I cringe at the suggestion that equality of opportunity suffices as a conception of economic justice. All too often real injustices are rationalized by claiming victims had equal opportunities but either failed, or chose not to make the best of them. Again, Sen himself may never fall victim to this ruse, but in the absence of a clear definition of what are equitable and inequitable *outcomes*, reducing economic justice to equality of opportunity is dangerous indeed.

Ironically, while I find Sen's critical work more intellectually compelling than his positive work, I think Sen will prove more influential as framer of a new approach to studying poverty and economic development than as a critic of mainstream economic theory, because of the difference in the receptivity of his two audiences. While Sen has destroyed intellectually a great deal of mainstream microeconomic theory and welfare economics, there are few practitioners in that field who *want* to hear what he has to say. They will remember Sen as a respected contributor to the task of refining axiomatic social choice theory – who inexplicably charged off on a fuzzy-headed political campaign. Economists such as Robert Pollack, who complained in an op-ed article in the *Wall Street Journal* the day after Sen was awarded the Nobel Prize that the Swedish Academy had erred terribly in honoring an "establishment leftist" with "muddleheaded views," are unlikely to hear what Sen has to say about the vacuity of mainstream welfare economics, much less take it to heart. Unfortunately it is the likes of Robert Pollack who dominate the field where, in my opinion, Sen did his most intellectually compelling work. On the other hand, the field of development economics is notorious for harboring self-styled "do-gooders" who are well aware that a single-minded focus on increasing GDP per capita is often counterproductive to economic development in any meaningful sense of the phrase. By pointing out all the ways that GDP per capita fails to capture economic progress, by insisting that economic progress for those at the bottom should count for more than further accumulation for those at the top, by shifting the focus from goods to whether the economy is making it possible for people to *do* more things they want to do, by emphasizing the complexity of economic development and wrapping it in the popular banner of freedom, Sen preaches to a receptive audience of development economists, staffers of charitable NGOs, and lower-level professionals who silently disagree with their superiors at the World Bank and IMF. For the most part this audience cares little if his new grand theory of economic development is intellectually airtight, or even if it resolves any long-standing difficulties in the field, as long as it affords them cover when they reject the strait-jacket of neoliberalism. Not that I object to using Sen's intellectual and professional credentials to battle neoliberalism. Far from it. Even if the rhetoric of entitlements, capacities, and development as freedom does little to untie any of the intellectual Gordian knots in development economics, as long as it throws sand into the wheels of the neoliberal juggernaut attempting to maximize the commercialization of human life and the natural environment, it is quite useful indeed.

NOTES

1. Herbert Gintis made many similar arguments at the same time ("Alienation and Power: Toward a Radical Welfare Economics", PhD Dissertation, Harvard University 1969, and "Welfare Criteria with Endogenous Preferences," *International Economic Review*, June 1974). Unlike Sen, however, Gintis' work received little attention because he had not previously established his reputation as a top theorist by refining mainstream theory, and because at the time he was an outspoken critic of capitalism.
2. See Robin Hahnel, "Endogenous Preferences: The Institutionalist Connection," in Amitava Dutt and Kenneth Jameson, eds, *Crossing the Mainstream* (Notre Dame, Ind.: University of Notre Dame Press, 2001).
3. See Robin Hahnel and Michael Albert, *Quiet Revolution in Welfare Economics* (Princeton: Princeton University Press, 1991).
4. *Ibid.*, chapter 6.
5. *Ibid.*, chapters 7,8 and 9.
6. See John Rawls, *A Theory of Justice* (Cambridge, Mass.: Harvard University Press, 1971).
7. See chapter 2, Robin Hahnel, *The ABCs of Political Economy: A Modern Approach* (London: Pluto Press, forthcoming).

NOTES ON CONTRIBUTORS

Carl Boggs is Professor of Social Science at National University in Los Angeles. He has written extensively on contemporary social and political theory, social movements, and political sociology. Among his many books have been two on Gramsci; his latest book is *The End of Politics: Corporate Power and the Public Sphere* (2000).

Douglas Dowd began to teach at U.C. Berkeley in 1950, thence to Cornell University for many years, thence back to the San Francisco area, where he resumed teaching at U.C. (both Berkeley and Santa Cruz), and in the California State University (San Francisco and San Jose), and also taught for ten years at the Johns Hopkins Univ. Center in Bologna, Italy. Among recent books are *Blues for America: A Critique, A Lament, and Some Memories* (1997), *Against the Conventional Wisdom: A Primer for Current Economic Controversies and Proposals* (1997), and *Capitalism and Its Economics: A Critical History* (2000). Now retired, he holds community classes in the SF Bay area.

John Bellamy Foster is Professor of Sociology at the University of Oregon. He is Coeditor of both *Monthly Review* and of *Organization and Environment*. His most recent book is *Marx's Ecology: Materialism and Nature* (2000). Among his many books are *The Vulnerable Planet: A Short Economic History of the Environment* (1993, 1999), *The Theory of Monopoly Capitalism: An Elaboration of Marxian Political Economy* (1986) and *The Faltering Economy: The Problem of Accumulation Under Monopoly Capitalism* (1984). He has published numerous articles in both academic and popular journals.

Robin Hahnel is Professor of Economics at the American University, Washington, D.C., and has served as visiting professor or economist in Cuba, Peru, and England. His most recent book is *Panic Rules! Everything You Need to Know About* *the Global Economy* (1999). He has written several books with Michael Albert, most relevantly for present purposes, *Quiet Revolution in Welfare Economics* and *The Political Economy of Participatory Economics* (1990, 1991), and, as well, numerous scholarly and popular essays.

Michael Keaney, a Scot, is a Lecturer in Economics and Finance at Mercuria Business School, Vantaa, Finland. He has published articles and reviews in the *Journal of Economic Issues, Review of Radical Political Economics, International Journal of Social Economics, Critical Sociology* and other journals. He is the editor of and contributor to *Economist with a Public Purpose: Essays in Honour of John Kenneth Galbraith* (Routledge, 2001).

Michael Lebowitz is Professor of Economics at Simon Fraser University, Vancouver, Canada. He is an editor of *Studies in Political Economy*, a contributing editor to *Science & Society*, and a member of the advisory board of *Historical Materialism*. His book *Beyond Capital: Marx's Political Economy of the Working Class* (1992, now being revised for republication) explores the side of Marx's theory not developed in *Capital*. Among his many articles in scholarly journals are "Analytical Marxism and the Marxian Theory of Crisis," and "Kornai and the Vanguard Mode of Production," both in the *Cambridge Journal of Economics* (1994, 1999). He is currently at work on a book provionally entitled *The Socialist Economy and the Vanguard Mode of Production*.

Frederic S. Lee has taught at U.C. Riverside (CA) and Roosevelt University (NY) in the USA, and at De Montfort University in England. He has recently joined the economics faculty at the University of Missouri-Kansas City. What all those teaching posts have had in common was one or more faculty members with a strong interest in heterodox-Post Keynesian economic courses and programs. He has written many articles in the PK framework (on full cost pricing, on PK production and cost theory, and PK industrial organization), and a book on PK price theory that received the Gunnar Myrdal Prize. In addition he has written many articles regarding various PK economists, in the USA and the UK, appearing in various professional journals. Among others of his recent works, are five chapters in a book on the late Alfred Eichner and on Joan Robinson (both important in the evolution of the PK school) and PK economics.

INDEX